LONGMAN L

r before

Volpone

Ben Johnson

Editor: Iain Veitch

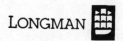

LONGMAN

Longman Literature

Series editor: Roy Blatchford

Plays

Alan Ayckbourn **Absurd Person Singular** 0 582 06020 6
Ad de Bont **Mirad, a Boy from Bosnia** 0 582 24949 X
Oliver Goldsmith **She Stoops to Conquer** 0 582 25397 7
Henrik Ibsen **Three plays: The Wild Duck, Ghosts** and **A Doll's House** 0 582 24948 1
Ben Jonson **Volpone** 0 582 25408 6
Christopher Marlowe **Doctor Faustus** 0 582 25409 4
Arthur Miller **An Enemy of the People** 0 582 09717 7
J B Priestley **An Inspector Calls** 0 582 06012 5
Terence Rattigan **The Winslow Boy** 0 582 06019 2
Jack Rosenthal **Wide-Eyed and Legless** 0 582 24950 3
Willy Russell **Educating Rita** 0 582 06013 3
 Shirley Valentine 0 582 08173 4
Peter Shaffer **Equus** 0 582 09712 6
 The Royal Hunt of the Sun 0 582 06014 1
Bernard Shaw **Arms and the Man** 0 582 07785 0
 The Devil's Disciple 0 582 25410 8
 Pygmalion 0 582 06015 X
 Saint Joan 0 582 07786 9
R B Sheridan **The Rivals** and **The School of Scandal** 0 582 25396 9
Oscar Wilde **The Importance of Being Earnest** 0 582 07784 2

Longman Literature Shakespeare

Series editor: Roy Blatchford

A Midsummer Night's Dream 0 582 08833 X (paper)
 0 582 24590 7 (cased)
As You Like It 0 582 23661 4 (paper)
Hamlet 0 582 09720 7 (paper)
Henry IV Part 1 0 582 23660 6 (paper)
Henry V 0 582 22584 1 (paper)
Julius Caesar 0 582 08828 3 (paper)
 0 582 24589 3 (cased)
King Lear 0 582 09718 5 (paper)
Macbeth 0 582 08827 5 (paper)
 0 582 24592 3 (cased)
The Merchant of Venice 0 582 08835 6 (paper)
 0 582 24593 1 (cased)
Othello 0 582 09719 3 (paper)
Richard III 0 582 23663 0 (paper)
Romeo and Juliet 0 582 08836 4 (paper)
 0 582 24591 5 (cased)
The Tempest 0 582 22583 3 (paper)
Twelfth Night 0 582 08834 8 (paper)

Other titles in the Longman Literature series are listed on page 322.

Contents

The writer on writing

Who was Ben Jonson?

A reading of The Epistle at the opening of **Volpone** appears to give a clear picture of the character of Ben Jonson: a classical scholar, moralistic in outlook, who viewed his contemporaries as being corrupt and believed that it was his role as a poet to educate, and so improve upon human nature. In other words, the type of arid, tedious philosopher which A-level students frequently complain of having to study.

However, a brief glance at Jonson's life reveals that his personality was far more complex; and that far from demonstrating the intellectual detachment he propounded, he was more prone to react emotionally to situations. It is no surprise then that much of his life was spent at odds with those in power.

Little is known of his early years, although it is clear that he came from humble beginnings. His natural father died before he was born and when his mother remarried, it was to a bricklayer. Jonson was apprenticed into his step-father's trade when he left Westminster School and, despite dedicating **Volpone** to Oxford and Cambridge, he never actually attended university. We can only assume that his great scholarship came from a voracious appetite for reading and a desire to improve upon his own position.

He volunteered to join the English army and fought in the Low Countries, killing a man in close combat, a feat of which he remained proud throughout his life. On his return home, he became an actor and then graduated to writing his own plays. His early work has not survived but it is known that his first play was deemed to be seditious and led to him being imprisoned for a brief spell, not for the last time.

In 1598, he wrote **Everyman and his Humour**, an immediate success in London. Typically Jonson did not enjoy this as he was once more in jail, this time for killing a fellow actor, Gabriel Spencer, in a duel. Although the crime was a capital offence, he escaped execution by converting to Catholicism and claiming clerical rights. How he carried this off is not clear, but the records show that his punishment was reduced to confiscation of all his goods and being branded on the thumb with the letter 'T'.

On his release, Jonson began a war of words with his contemporaries, Marston and Dekker, which lasted for much of his career: even his condemnation in this text of those who use their art for slander is an obtuse attack upon them! An inclination to outspokenness led once more to trouble in his next work, **Eastward Ho**! (1605), in that the play's satire on the Scots was interpreted as an attack upon James I: a spell behind bars again resulted. Reputed associations with the Gunpowder Plot conspirators, no doubt given weight by Jonson's past record, led to him being impeached as a Catholic traitor in 1606, a potentially serious charge which was quickly dropped.

Despite these private and public skirmishes, Jonson wrote four great comedies: **Volpone** (1605), **The Alchemist** (1610), **Bartholemew Fair** (1614) and **The Devil is an Ass** (1616). He enjoyed considerable success as a dramatist and grew in prosperity and reputation, so much so that, for a time, he was even a favourite at the royal court. Sadly, in his later years, despite being relatively prolific in writing masques, his muse largely deserted him and he died, poor and ill, in 1637. His early reputation was such that he was buried in Westminster Abbey.

A scholar but also a fighter, a man as happy with the sword as with the pen, Jonson retains the power to amuse and shock which he had almost four hundred years ago. His aim might be to educate but, given his character, it is guaranteed that the lesson will not be a dull one!

His poetic beliefs

In the dedicatory Epistle at the beginning of **Volpone**, Jonson gives a very clear picture of his poetic beliefs. For him, the role of poetry had been defined by the poets of Ancient Greece, and restated lucidly by the writers of the Italian Renaissance. He believed that the role of the writer was

> to inform young men to all good disciplines, inflame grown men to all great virtues, keep old men in their best and supreme state, or, as they decline to childhood, recover them to their first strength

lines 25–8

It is important to understand these ideas when approaching Jonson's work because they enable us to see that his was a classical model of comedy, one whose aim was to instruct as well as to amuse. Like Sir Philip Sidney, he believed that:

> Comedy is an imitation of the common errors of life, which he (the dramatist) representeth in the most ridiculous and scornful sort that may be so as it is impossible that any beholder can be content to be such a one.

Sir Philip Sidney, **Apologia for Poetry**

In other words, he wanted his audience to be amused by his characters but also to feel uneasy, to recognise their own faults.

Jonson scorned the contemporary fashions of slapstick and crude farce and instead championed the medium of satire, one which allowed him to teach through generalities, creating almost caricatures of Greed, Lust and Ignorance, rather than attack living people; his target was to improve all humanity rather than individual malefactors and that is why his voice still speaks to us today.

A notable feature of Jonson's art is the sheer weight of learning that his plays embody. Numerous references to ancient philosophy and myth, to historical figures and to religion adorn the dialogue, making the lessons given universal. This style of writing is again classical in nature, in that the writer values not only the plot but also the language with which it is developed; as Jonson said, his greatest desire is to

> ... restore her [poetry] to her primitive habit, feature and majesty, and render her worthy to be embraced and kissed of all the great and master-spirits of our world.

Nothing annoyed him more than the 'solecisms', 'bold prolepsies', 'racked metaphors' and 'impropriety of phrase' of his fellow dramatists, whose sole aim was to make money regardless of the cost to their artistic integrity.

To a modern reader this must seem both alienating and daunting: how can we be amused by a man whose models and language are so removed from our experience? The answer is that breathing through Jonson's work is an exuberance, a vitality of spirit which retains its power to thrill. We may not appreciate every reference, but the beauty of the poetry is clear; some of the allusions which characters make may escape us, but their motives are obvious, their frailties exposed; some of the most clever wordplay may be above us, but the vast body of the comedy is as funny now as it was then. As is so characteristic of his own life, Jonson took classical learning and imbued into it a tremendous energy. The audience's role now is as it has always been: to sit back, enjoy and learn.

What was England like in his lifetime?

Jonson's life encompassed a period of immense change, economical, social and political, and this gave him a wealth of material to satirise.

Elizabeth I's reign had seen a consolidation of Protestantism as the national religion. Catholics were persecuted ruthlessly for their beliefs and had their lands confiscated to add to the royal coffers. Internationally, relationships with the great Catholic power of Spain were tense and broke out into open enmity, resulting in the attempted invasion by the Armada in 1588. The consequence of this domestic and foreign strife was a growth in the government's belief that some of the population were agents provocateurs, working within the state for its overthrow. An intricate secret service had been set up by Queen Elizabeth I to investigate such claims and subsequently all those reported as having unorthodox beliefs were questioned, often under torture.

The insecurity of those in power was further heightened by the Earl of Essex's revolt and then by the accession of James I in 1603. He was from north of the border and relationships between the two countries had been strained, particularly as Scotland had harboured Elizabeth's traitorous sister, Mary. His popularity was by no means widespread in his new kingdom and he set about improving this by extending royal patronage to his friends and potential supporters. The result was a rapid extension of the honours given, a trend satirised by Jonson through the character of Sir Politic Would-be. Such an attack was characteristic of a man keen to highlight weakness wherever he saw it, and helps us to understand why he was constantly in trouble in a regime whose eyes were turned inward looking for potential traitors.

Society itself was also undergoing rapid transition. Economically, Stuart England was an expanding capitalist centre, leading to the rise of the professional classes as a powerful body. This augmented a trend begun by the Tudor monarchs to give political clout to Parliament, although in their time this was largely illusory and used to put the blame on to others for unpopular measures. Notions of feudalism had largely broken down, bringing a challenge to traditional views of life which Jonson despised. He believed that the new order with its commercialised exploitation of the weakest, was amoral, reducing human activity to the level of the jungle, an idea he developed in **Volpone**.

Finally, the age was one in which learning was prized and, subsequently, huge advances were made in knowledge. The Italian Renaissance had led to a rediscovery of classical study and a new value being placed upon scholarship which had carried through into

Elizabethan times. Scientific advances, for example, the invention of the telescope, had led to a reappraisal of human understanding of the world but also to a reactionary hardening of religious dogma by the Church. An example of this was the growth in England of an extreme form of Protestantism – Puritanism – which denounced all pleasure-giving activities, including dancing, singing and theatre-going, as sinful and called for their prohibition. Its narrow mindedness would later lead to the mass slaughter of the Salem 'witches' in America, but, at this time, it found favour with a government suspicious of individuality: Jonson's opinion of such bigotry is clear in his sporadic jibes at Puritans in **Volpone**.

Here we have then a scholar intent on instructing through satire at a time when thought was encouraged, dissent persecuted: increasingly, the turbulence of Jonson's life becomes understandable.

How was his work received?

A history of the critical reception of **Volpone** shows that by no means every age has seen it as a sparkling gem in the crown of English literature.

Initially it was acclaimed as a masterpiece, with Samuel Pepys declaring that it was, 'a most excellent play; the best I think I ever saw', but in the seventeenth century it was largely dismissed. Congreve complained about the lampooning of the deafness of Corbaccio, feeling that it was contrary to the aims set out in the Epistle, whilst Dryden found the final act contrived, and the ending unsatisfactory in terms of the classical model Jonson was purporting to follow. Eighteenth-century critics also found the play to be flawed, regarding the sub-plot as unnecessary and the plot as a whole, unrealistic: the figure of Corbaccio and the ending were picked out again for particular scorn. The result was that by the nineteenth century, **Volpone** was largely ignored.

It was T S Eliot who rescued the play from obscurity at the beginning of the twentieth century. He pointed to the beauty of the verse and attacked all those who saw the play as unrealistic, arguing that it was never intended to be true to life. Eliot's point was that Jonson had written a dramatic fable, one in which naturalism was sacrificed for both the needs of comedy and the desire to make a moral point. Quite correctly, he concluded that, when viewed in this way, the play was a success; that far from being contrived, it had a 'unity of inspiration that radiates into plot and personages alike.'

Although subsequent critics have echoed their predecessors' unease at the sub-plot, and particularly the episode in which Sir Politic hides in the tortoise shell, all have agreed with Eliot that **Volpone** is a superb example of Jacobean comedy, a masterpiece which deserves its place in the nation's canon.

Introduction

Sources

Jonson made no attempt to mask either his appreciation of classical literature or his willingness to borrow from it: such imitation was an accepted part of Jacobean drama. From the Ancient Greeks, he derived the notion of a set of laws governing comedy: that its aim should be educational and that it should have consistency (unity) in time, place and action. Unity in time meant that the events should be a continuous sequence, mirroring a similar interlude in real life; unity of place meant that only one location should be used; and of action, that the plot should proceed without any hindrance.

Another aspect of the tradition which he displayed in **Volpone** was a storyline of legacy-hunters being duped, and thus revealed as fools. The use of a witty parasite was an ancient device as was the practice of lampooning professional men, although Jonson took this to new heights with the creation of Mosca. This suited the dramatist's own prejudices, as the relentless satire on lawyers, embodied in the character of Voltore, demonstrates.

Jonson's use of classical techniques is most clearly shown in Act 2, scene 3, in which Corvino describes the piazza scene in terms of the characters created by the Renaissance movement, the *commedia dell'arte*: here the dramatist is openly tipping his hat to those he has used as his models.

However, to see Jonson as a mere mimic would be to underestimate his dramatic techniques. There is no known source for the story of **Volpone**; it is a creation of the dramatist's imagination. Although he adapted Aesop's fable of the fox and the crow, and acknowledged this by constant reference to it in the text, he did so with ingenuity, peopling the simplistic story with a host of foolish victims, as well as two skilled predators. The result is that he was not only able to exploit a greater range of comic opportunities than the original represents, but also to explore greed in a far more complex way.

His invention led him to subvert the very traditions he was imitating, to bend them to meet his own needs. In this way, the classical law of unity of action was ignored by the inclusion of the sub-plot of the Politic Would-bes, one which mirrors, and thus sheds light upon, the main plot, as well as allowing Jonson to satirise the behaviour of the English abroad.

Similarly, a traditional 'happy' ending would have been at odds with the main thrust of the plot so Jonson chose instead a climax which is almost tragic in its nature, tracing the downfall and death of the lead character rather than his salvation. The forces of virtue seem weak when juxtaposed with the vitality of the corruption on show and although the ending purports to demonstrate the workings of Providence, one is left feeling more that evil has destroyed itself by its over-reaching nature.

Jonson recognises all of these departures in his Epistle, apologising for them and, quite correctly, stating that they were due to 'industry' on his part: they were the result of a conscious decision by a dramatist who valued tradition but also saw the need to build upon it; to imitate creatively in order to develop comic technique; to assimilate what was best of old methods rather than just to ape them thoughtlessly.

- As you read **Volpone**, note how it is true to the laws of unity in time and place. What does each bring to the drama?

- Research the fable of the fox and the crow. This will enable you to appreciate Jonson's skill in adapting it.

- Research what is meant – in classical terms – by 'comedy' and 'tragedy'. How do the endings of each differ?

Themes

Jonson believed that the move in society to capitalism would bring with it a debasement of human nature; that the civilised values which he put so much store by were in danger of being subsumed in a tide of greed, as people became motivated by more mercenary desires than the urge to do good. He intended **Volpone** to be a vehicle for his criticism of this trend and thus created a jungle setting for it, a self-contained world which was peopled exclusively by predators and their prey. It was his belief that man was indeed reducing himself to animalistic behaviour because of his greed, that he was entering into this corruption willingly and would lose his virtue in doing so. For this reason, the characters of the play are largely monsters, creatures dressing up their bestial desires in the garb of civilised speech and action.

It follows that, along with the greed, a key theme in the play is the difference between appearance and reality. The characters' names suggest that they are players in a fable and act as labels to show their inner corruption (see page 12). Corvino, Corbaccio and Voltore, all upstanding members of Venetian society, all concerned about the failing health of a dying man, are nothing more than birds of prey waiting to pick his corpse clean; Mosca, the loyal, loving servant, is as parasitic as his name suggests, in that he feeds off the corruption around him and will happily ingest his host if the occasion presents itself; his master, Volpone, not only recognises his bestial association, but basks in it, dressing in furs and wallowing in the urge to deceive which is at the heart of his personality. All prowl around the stage in an animalistic way, rarely walking, and all are able to change their behaviour startlingly quickly, demanding that the audience must question all that they say and do: irony abounds.

- Identify the different bestial 'tags' given to characters.
- As you read the play:
  - look for how fitting these names are. Does each character act according to his/her defined nature?

— identify speeches in which characters use animalistic imagery and distinguish between when they do this consciously and unconsciously;

— which characters use irony deliberately and what does this show about them?

Setting

Jonson's choice of location was fitting in many ways. Given the restrictions at home, and the tendency of the authorities to see treachery where none was intended, where better to set the play than abroad, in Venice – a city famous for its mercantile prosperity, its treasure houses; in other words in a city which was a magnified reflection of London's aspirations? Its reputation for artistic patronage, humanist scholarship, deriving from its classical background, and Renaissance grandeur served Jonson's purpose because he wanted to show that if vice could thrive there, the centre of human excellence, then it could thrive anywhere. By exposing the moral vacuity at the heart of such an illustrious city, he hoped to warn England of the true nature of the fate it seemed so intent on seeking.

In choosing Italy, Jonson was not only paying homage to the source of his muse but also playing to the prejudices of his audience. To the Jacobeans, this nation was reputed to be rife with exotic crime, its people faithful disciples of the teaching of Machiavelli that human frailty could be exploited for gain by those cunning and courageous enough to do so. This is exactly what we see on stage.

Venice, therefore, allowed Jonson to place his audience in a world familiar enough for them to recognise their vices but too unfamiliar for them to be able to interpret satire as slander. And, of course, his great contemporary Shakespeare had not been shy in using similar Italian locations for his plays.

The role of the audience

Volpone marks a departure from the norms of Jacobean comedy in that it lacks a satirical commentator, an actor whose role is to interpret character and actions for the audience in order to show them the dramatist's standpoint. The closest it gets to this is the character of Peregrine in the sub-plot. Jonson's purpose in this omission was to involve the audience actively in the drama, to make them less passive in their viewing of the entertainment by forcing them to make judgements about the actions of the central protagonists. In this way he aimed to force us to recognise that, in respect of Volpone and his parasite, our sympathies are at odds with our moral values: we view their fall with a certain degree of sorrow because we see a removal of wit, intelligence and energy from the world; at the same time, we recognise that they represent an evil which must be defeated. Our fascination with them is a warning to us of how attractive corruption is: we can be taken in by it as easily as the legacy-hunters we despise are.

Characterisation

Volpone

It is easy to be fooled by Volpone's opening blasphemous eulogy to his treasure into thinking that avarice is the key to his personality. Undoubtedly, it is an important facet of his character – references to it stray even into the passionate appraisal of Celia as being 'bright as gold' – but its possession by no means dominates his thoughts; he is as happy to spend his wealth lavishly as he is to acquire it.

Volpone's chief motivation, his *raison d'être*, is constantly to show to himself that he is better than other men; that in a world of petty greed, his is an appetite of almost divine stature. For this reason, he constantly drives himself on to greater excesses, risking all time and time again to prove that he can outwit any opponent: he is a fox who, paradoxically, enjoys every aspect of the chase.

In many respects, Volpone has all the qualities of the 'Renaissance man': he is an accomplished performer and mimic, a skilled poet and a classical scholar. He has a vast intelligence, a lively wit and a vitality which places him above the norm, and yet all of these qualities have been perverted by a fatal flaw: self love. This leads him to spend his time in Machiavellian plotting rather than in exercising his mind for the good of humanity. For him, acquisition, be it of goods or people, is the proof of his genius. Such egotism is also his Achilles' heel because it leads him to be so intoxicated with himself that he is blind to the threat which Mosca poses, even when the change in the balance of their relationship is obvious. Ultimately, the weakness will lead to his destruction because he will choose to suffer at the hands of the court rather than allow his parasite the satisfaction of beating him.

It is wrong to see Volpone as having been corrupted over a passage of time, as some commentators suggest. The choice to be amoral was one he made consciously and this can be seen by the way he not only dismisses virtue as being a source of weakness, but also plays with notions of what it actually constitutes. In the seduction scene, he derides Celia's pleas of constancy by showing that her marriage to the impotent Corvino is a sham. Arguing that it cannot be virtuous to accept such an unnatural state of affairs, he offers to free her, using images which suggest that his is the natural passion. It is only her unyielding constancy which shows that this righteousness is another mask, that behind these sentiments the fox lurks, ready to resort to violence if his charm fails.

This scene, and the one in which he adores his gold, show that he is a man who glories in his own corruption; that, having surveyed those who purport to be 'good' and found only weakness and greed, he has chosen a criminal life because he has no fear of retribution, divine or otherwise. He is a man who, foolishly, perceives himself to be a god because all around him are such minnows.

In this respect, he performs a critical function in the play. The images of decay which surround him, and the freakish nature of his bastard offspring, leave us in no doubt that he is evil, but he is a catalyst for, rather than the cause of, much of the corruption which we see. The professional classes – represented by Corbaccio, Corvino, Voltore and, to some extent, the Avocatori – were riddled with self-interest long before they were caught in his snare and even the forces of virtue were not unblemished. Despite her pleas of faithfulness, we see a coquettish side to Celia's character in her dropping of the handkerchief to the mountebank, and Bonario, in his early dealings with Mosca, shows himself to be somewhat priggish. The truth is that Volpone exists in a Venice which is inhabited by scavengers, parasites and fools, one in which natural bonds count for nothing in the pursuit of gold, and he is merely a magnified version of these vices. When comparing him to the slow-wittedness of those who surround him, we, like the character himself, are dazzled by his magnificence.

- This is a brief introduction to the character of Volpone. Isolate what you consider to be the key points and when you are reading the text, collect evidence to flesh them out. In particular, look for occasions where he is:
  - a skilled actor;
  - an accomplished poet;
  - an ironic commentator on his own actions.

Mosca

Mosca fulfils a dual role in the play. He is the parasite of classical drama, exploiting the weakness of others in order to prosper and glorifying in his ability to do so. However, he is also, in many respects, the devil of the medieval morality plays, exposing corruption and feeding men the opportunities to wallow in the vice that will damn them. He gets Corvino, a jealous husband, to act as a pimp for his own wife, Corbaccio to disinherit the son he purports to love and Voltore to abuse the notions of truth which should be at the very heart of his profession: in all, he simply motivates their greed into breaking natural bonds. He has seen through the society of Venice and, in his pursuit of pleasure, acts almost as a scourge, exposing evil and, in Act 5, passing sentence upon the guilty before dismissing them.

The key to Mosca's success is that he has understood that men see what they want to, blinding themselves to the truth of situations in order to shape a reality more suited to their own desires. He thrives initially because his is a very clear view: he recognises the truth about his station and is contented in it. However, like his master, he becomes intoxicated with his own success and attempts to rise higher, thus over-reaching himself. At the end, he is defeated by the very weakness he has exploited in others, self-delusion, in that he chooses to ignore how badly Volpone will take defeat.

- How do Mosca's motivations differ from Volpone's? Does this difference play a significant factor in his downfall?
- In many ways, Mosca is as accomplished as his master in intellect and wit. As you read the text, collect evidence of him being:
  — a skilled manipulator of situations;
  — an ironic commentator on the action.
- Throughout the day, the balance of the relationship between Volpone and Mosca changes. Trace this change and explain why it happens.

The Politic Would-bes

Because the play is so long, directors frequently cut the sub-plot, and so omit completely the character of Sir Politic Would-be. This may fit the expedient needs of live theatre but it damages the unity of the play because it removes the foil of the major character. In some respects the knight is a vehicle for satire on the English abroad, and the strange illusions they have about foreigners. More importantly, his career mirrors that of Volpone, travestying his actions and foreshadowing his ultimate defeat. Such parallels are clear in his schemes to get rich quick and endless intriguing, contrasting with the more skilled manipulations of the magnifico, and, subtly, in the substitute for quarantine measures he offers the City fathers, a cure reminiscent of the mountebank's. In all, he appears ludicrously inept, moving towards revelation and ruin, a burlesque of the maestro's own fate. His role is to remind us that folly is closely related to more heinous sins.

Lady Politic's key characteristic is her superficiality, a trait she shares with the legacy-hunters. Although she is an amateur in a world of professional fraudsters, her very ineptitude allows her to turn the tables on Volpone, in that her garrulousness reduces him to a quivering wreck. In a scene which is a comic reversal of the more violent one to follow, she attempts a clumsy seduction and is only thwarted by the arrival of Mosca. Her parting gift, a cap of her own making, is as crude an attempt at solicitation as her physical one and illustrates clearly her role: to highlight the greater avarice of the suitors by mirroring their actions. Interestingly, in her affected free thinking and subsequent promiscuous behaviour, she is also a foil to the virtue of Celia, although the parallels are a little too strained to work convincingly.

Together the Politic Would-bes act as a warning to the English. Comfort cannot be taken in their relative innocence in the crimes committed because they have gone to great trouble to involve themselves in the intrigues around them and have failed only because of their own stupidity. They represent the thin edge of the wedge which is the thriving corruption of the Venetian citizens.

- Trace the career of Sir Politic in the play and explain why his name is so ironically fitting. In particular, contrast what he would be and what he is.
- Look at Lady Would-be's character and actions and decide what she brings to the play in terms of comedy.

Celia and Bonario

Celia and Bonario represent virtue in Venice and, as such, are seen for the most part to be fragile and out of place, although their faith in divine justice appears to be rewarded at the end of the play. As an audience, we feel we should sympathise with both because they are betrayed by those they have most reason to trust, yet we never wholly identify with them. Part of the reason for this is that their characterisation is so two-dimensional when compared to the rest, but also because we are deliberately kept at a distance from them by the dramatist.

Celia is seen to be subjected to horrendous abuse by her husband before becoming the pawn in a repugnant scheme which results in her almost being violently raped: an horrific sequence of events and yet in her melodramatic vows of constancy and subsequent pathetic reactions in court, she provokes our laughter rather than our sympathy. Similarly, Bonario is disinherited by his father through no fault of his own and goes on to commit the only selfless act of the play in his rescue of Celia, yet his subsequent attitudinising, characterised by archaic heroic language, makes him a figure of fun.

Jonson chose to undercut even the actions of the virtuous with irony to detach us from them. His aim was to satirise all, to show that a sentimental view of righteousness is out of place when evil is so virulent; that modern times require more than passive resistance or posing.

- Is Celia a satisfactory character or is she poorly drawn? Studied with Lady Politic, would you say Jonson had a problem creating female characters?
- Look at the other forces of virtue, the Avocatori. Do they give the audience a greater reason for optimism or are they also inadequate in the face of the evil represented by Volpone and Mosca?

The language of the play

Volpone moves at such a swift pace that it is often easy to underestimate the linguistic skill evident within it. Written in blank verse, its characters' language consistently matches the situations they find themselves in. (Their linguistic dexterity is, of course, Jonson's.) A clear view of this can be seen if one looks at three contrasting scenes. As a mountebank, Volpone mimics perfectly the patter of the street-seller, passing off falsities as truisms and drawing the audience, both on and off stage, to him by the outrageousness of his sales pitch. Minutes later, he is a love poet, enticing Celia into adultery with an Olympian vision of the pleasures he can offer her. Later, the dramatist captures perfectly the language of the courtroom as Voltore dazzles all with his legal rhetoric, convincing the judges that palpable absurdities are facts and so ensuring that injustice triumphs. All three scenes involve the use of language to deceive, yet no two are similar.

It is a mark of his genius that Jonson, who prized rhetorical skill above all else, is able to warn his audience against even this. Volpone and Mosca show themselves to be well versed in classical learning yet prove that this can be perverted to dupe others, whilst Voltore shows that purity in language usage can often be deceptive.

Irony abounds as characters consciously engage in the type of double-speak which Orwell was to formalise three hundred years later in *Nineteen Eighty-Four*, or unconsciously reveal their inner selves through their speech. A notable example of the latter is in the trial scene, in which the bestial characters denounce Bonario and Celia as a 'monster', 'a chameleon' and a 'crocodile', charging them with crimes beyond their scope but well within the capabilities of the accusers.

It is by no means vital that a modern audience understands all of the language in the play but to be blind to many of its nuances would be to enjoy only half of its true quality.

- Choose a dominant motif in the play (e.g. disease, feeding, gold) and collect examples of its usage. Discuss how it is used by characters and what it shows about them.
- Collect examples of where characters consciously use irony and where their speech betrays them. Volpone and Mosca are useful for the former, Lady Politic for the latter.

The ending

Jonson's skill in structuring the play can be seen if one studies the ending. It has been prepared for carefully, in that its structure of crisis, panic and resolution is one which has been repeated throughout. One has only to look at Volpone's despair after the mountebank scene, and the subsequent plot to win Celia; his panic at the attempted seduction by Lady Would-be and subsequent rescue; and his fatalism at the likely consequences of his attack upon Celia leading to the trial scene, in which justice is perverted in his favour, in order to see this. In each instance, the character has flirted increasingly with disaster and so is now seen to be defeated rather than victorious at the resolution.

The ending is a finely crafted piece yet has been subjected to criticism because it does not follow the classical model in which characters recognise their sins and seek forgiveness; no one in *Volpone* expresses any sorrow at their actions and the notion of reformation is not introduced. Instead all are subjected to punishments which suit the nature of their crime; thus, the Politic Would-bes, guilty of folly, are dealt with less severely than those whose vices have affected others. However, although Bonario benefits from his honesty, Celia is almost certainly worse off, being left not only in a bankrupt marriage but also indirectly to share the public scorn aimed at her husband; one can imagine her attracting the sympathy of the ordinary citizens but also being the subject of ribaldry concerning the cuckold who never was.

Jonson's aim in ending the piece on such a dark note was in keeping with his aim for the play as a whole. He wanted to leave his audience feeling uneasy, to challenge their sentimental notions by showing that in the modern world there is no such thing as a truly happy ending. In this way, although Providence is recognised as the force which restored order, one cannot but feel that it is the evil characters themselves who have been responsible for their downfall: they were defeated not by the forces of virtue but by their own overweaning desires.

Similarly, one can take no real comfort in the type of justice given because it reflects the class snobbery which has allowed corruption to flourish. Mosca is not dealt with most severely because he was the most guilty but because he is the poorest in terms of social status and, one cannot help feeling, because he tricked the Avocatori into treating him like a gentleman. It follows that Jonson wanted us to see that the removal of Volpone and his parasite from the world does not necessarily mean it is a better place, because the conditions which allowed them to flourish – greed, frailty, stupidity – are still present. Volpone's final speech, a sardonic joke about his own fate, shows that the evil he represents is by no means so easily wiped out: even in defeat, its spirit remains, its ability to rob virtue of its victory by refusing to bow down to it.

- Look at the ending carefully and decide where you stand in the debate. Is it a fitting conclusion or does it show, as many argue, that Jonson was essentially disinterested at this stage and merely seeking to round the play off; that essentially he botched it?

A reminder

This introduction is intended to whet your appetite for the play and to set your mind working upon its meaning. It is by no means definitive nor will it serve as a substitute for your own involvement with the text. The play is a challenging one but can be deeply rewarding if you allow your intellect to be engaged by it. Above all, remember that it was intended to be performed and that nothing will help you to understand it more than to act out scenes, and so to see how they would look and sound on stage, or to go and see it performed. Only then will you truly tune into its comedy, and thus enjoy it in the way Jonson would have wanted.

Reading log

One of the easiest ways of keeping track of your reading is to keep a log book. This can be any exercise book or folder that you have to hand, but make sure you reserve it exclusively for reflecting on your reading, both at home and in school.

As you read the play, stop from time to time and think back over what you have read.

- Is there anything that puzzles you? Note down some questions that you might want to research, discuss with your friends or ask a teacher. Also note any quotations which strike you as important or memorable.

- Does your reading remind you of anything else you have read, heard or seen on TV or the cinema? Jot down what it is and where the similarities lie.

- Have you had any experiences similar to those occurring in the play? Do you find yourself identifying closely with one or more of the characters? Record this as accurately as you can.

- Do you find yourself really liking, or really loathing, any of the characters? What is it about them that makes you feel so strongly? Make notes that you can add to.

- Can you picture the locations and settings? Draw maps, plans, diagrams, drawings, in fact any doodle that helps you make sense of these things.

- Now and again try to predict what will happen next in the plot. Use what you already know of the playwright and the characters to help you do this. Later record how close you were and whether you were surprised at the outcome.

- Write down any feelings that you have about the play. Your reading log should help you to make sense of your own ideas alongside those of the playwright.

TO THE MOST NOBLE
AND MOST ÆQVALL
SISTERS

THE TWO FAMOVS VNIVERSITIES,

FOR THEIR LOVE
AND
ACCEPTANCE

SHEW'N TO HIS POEME
IN THE PRESENTATION:

BEN: IONSON

THE GRATEFVLL ACKNOWLEDGER
DEDICATES
BOTH IT, AND HIMSELFE.

There followes an *Epistle*, if
you dare venture on
the length.

¶

The dedication from the Quarto

Volpone
or
The Fox

The Epistle is in the form of a letter addressed to the universities of Oxford and Cambridge. It is a bitter attack on those contemporary dramatists who Jonson believed had debased the name of poetry by their shoddy workmanship. He felt that they had ignored the traditional role of the poet, as an instructor to mankind, in their pursuit of profit and were too willing to play to the rabble. Contemporary drama was more noted for obscenity than good poetry. In contrast, Jonson places his own plays as being works of art and pledges to do all in his power to expose the inferior practitioners to public ridicule.

1–3   **Never ... to it**   a man can never be so intelligent that he cannot improve further with the help of opportunities and friends.

5–6   **it behoves ... accidents**   it means that the wise always cultivate such aids.

9–10   **am studious ... act**   am careful to justify the good favour with which you have received my play.

10–11   **though ... satisfying**   though your good names should be enough.

14   **forehead**   strong belief.

14–17   **too-much license ... her**   too much credence has been given to bad poets with the result that much bad poetry is produced, so the whole art form is debased.

17–18   **But for their petulancy**   because of their cheek.

21–2   **asquint**   a biased way.

21–33   **For, if men ... rhetoric upon**   Jonson develops his belief that for a man to be a good poet, his nature must be virtuous. He believes that the poet has an important function in both instructing and elevating men's souls and thus the position should not be a target for abuse ('railing rhetoric').

The Epistle

Never (most equal sisters) had any man a wit so presently
excellent as that it could raise itself, but there must come
both matter, occasion, commenders, and favourers to it. If
this be true, and that the fortune of all writers doth daily
prove it, it behoves the careful to provide well toward   5
these accidents; and, having acquired them, to preserve
that part of reputation most tenderly, wherein the benefit
of a friend is also defended. Hence is it, that I now render
myself grateful, and am studious to justify the bounty of
your act, to which, though your mere authority were satis-   10
fying, yet (it being an age wherein poetry and the pro-
fessors of it hear so ill on all sides) there will a reason be
looked for in the subject. It is certain, nor can it with any
forehead be opposed, that the too-much licence of poetas-
ters in this time hath much deformed their mistress; that   15
every day their manifold and manifest ignorance doth
stick unnatural reproaches upon her. But for their petulancy it were an act of the greatest injustice either to let the
learned suffer, or so divine a skill (which indeed should
not be attempted with unclean hands) to fall under the   20
least contempt. For, if men will impartially, and not asquint, look toward the offices and function of a poet, they
will easily conclude to themselves the impossibility of any
man's being the good poet, without first being a good
man. He that is said to be able to inform young men to all   25
good disciplines, inflame grown men to all great virtues,
keep old men in their best and supreme state, or, as they
decline to childhood, recover them to their first strength;
that comes forth the interpreter and arbiter of nature, a
teacher of things divine no less than human, a master in   30
manners; and can alone (or with a few) effect the business
of mankind: this, I take him, is no subject for pride and
ignorance to exercise their railing rhetoric upon. But it

36 **inverted** he believes that modern writers are immoral in that they write only for the rewards it can bring.

42–3 **abortive features** ill-conceived plays.

45–6 **a more malicious slander** Jonson feels that a part, but not all, of his profession have fallen into disrepute. He is anxious to divorce himself from popular conceptions of playwrights/poets.

48 **profaneness** blasphemy.

49 **bawdry** obscenity.

50 **food** main substance.

51–4 **sharpness ... teeth** he complains that satire on his part is misinterpreted constantly for bitterness. Even his most recent play is seen as being too biting.

54 **politics** critics.

54–5 **what nation ... have provoked?** he denies insulting any actual person or country, although such jibes, particularly at James I, can be perceived in his play (e.g. the fact that Sir Politic has been knighted is a political criticism).

58 **allowed** passed by the censor.

59 **broad reproofs** indecent insults.

67–8 **made obnoxious to construction** made indecent by being wrongly interpreted.

69 **Application** the attempt to spot real people in fictitious characters.

will here be hastily answered, that the writers of these
days are other things; that not only their manners but   35
their natures are inverted; and nothing remaining with
them of the dignity of poet but the abused name, which
every scribe usurps; that now, especially in dramatic or
(as they term it) stage poetry, nothing but ribaldry, pro-
fanation, blasphemy, all licence of offence to God and   40
man, is practised. I dare not deny a great part of this (and
am sorry I dare not), because in some men's abortive features (and would they had never boasted the light) it is
over-true; but that all are embarked in this bold adventure
for hell is a most uncharitable thought, and, uttered, a   45
more malicious slander. For my particular, I can (and
from a most clear conscience) affirm that I have ever trem-
bled to think toward the least profaneness; have loathed
the use of such foul and unwashed bawdry as is now made
the food of the scene. And, howsoever I cannot escape   50
from some the imputation of sharpness, but that they will
say I have taken a pride or lust to be bitter, and not my
youngest infant but hath come into the world with all his
teeth, I would ask of these supercilious politics, what
nation, society, or general order, or state I have provoked?   55
What public person? Whether I have not (in all these)
preserved their dignity, as mine own person, safe? My
works are read, allowed (I speak of those that are entirely
mine) – look into them. What broad reproofs have I used?
Where have I been particular? Where personal? except to   60
a mimic, cheater, bawd, or buffoon – creatures (for their
insolencies) worthy to be taxed? Yet to which of these so
pointingly as he might not either ingenuously have con-
fessed or wisely dissembled his disease? But it is not
rumour can make men guilty, much less entitle me to   65
other men's crimes. I know that nothing can be so in-
nocently writ or carried, but may be made obnoxious to
construction; marry, whilst I bear mine innocence about
me, I fear it not. Application is now grown a trade with

73 *fames*   reputations.

74 *virulent malice*   Jonson believes that often the dramatist is guiltless of malice; it is the interpretation put on his work which has this purpose; i.e. the claim of slander is nothing more than a cover for slander.

75–80 **As for ... a rival**   Jonson disassociates himself from those who use their art to revive old scandals or to slander living people.

85 *antique relics of barbarism*   he understands why some, faced with plays which set out to insult, would rather theatre reverted back to simpler styles e.g. jesters and comic morality devils.

89 **Sibi ... odit**   (Latin) 'In satires, each man, though untouched, feels as if he were hurt, and, therefore, hates the entertainment.'

90–1 *lust in liberty*   delight in obscenity.

95 *solecisms*   grammatical errors.

96 *prolepses*   anachronisms.

racked   strained.

brothelry   obscenity.

101 *name*   the title of poet.

103–4 *vernaculous*   common.

many; and there are, that profess to have a key for the 70
deciphering of everything. But let wise and noble persons
take heed how they be too credulous, or give leave to these
invading interpreters to be over-familiar with their fames,
who cunningly and often utter their own virulent malice
under other men's simplest meanings. As for those that 75
will (by faults which charity hath raked up or common
honesty concealed) make themselves a name with the multitude, or (to draw their rude and beastly claps) care not
whose living faces they entrench with their petulant styles,
may they do it without a rival, for me – I choose rather to 80
live graved in obscurity than share with them in so preposterous a fame. Nor can I blame the wishes of those
severe and wiser patriots, who, providing the hurts these
licentious spirits may do in a state, desire rather to see
fools and devils and those antique relics of barbarism re- 85
trieved, with all other ridiculous and exploded follies, than
behold the wounds of private men, of princes, and nations.
For, as Horace makes Trebatius speak, among these,

   – *Sibi quisque timet, quamquam est intactus, et odit*

And men may justly impute such rages, if continued, to
the writer, as his sports. The increase of which lust in 90
liberty, together with the present trade of the stage, in all
their misc'line interludes, what learned or liberal soul
doth not already abhor? – where nothing but the filth of
the time is uttered, and that with such impropriety of
phrase, such plenty of solecisms, such dearth of sense, so 95
bold prolepses, so racked metaphors, with brothelry able
to violate the ear of a pagan, and blasphemy to turn the
blood of a Christian to water. I cannot but be serious in a
cause of this nature, wherein my fame and the reputations
of divers honest and learned are the question; when a 100
name so full of authority, antiquity, and all great mark, is
(through their insolence) become the lowest scorn of the
age; and those men subject to the petulancy of every vernaculous orator, that were wont to be the care of kings and

105 **rapt**   forced.

109 **arbitresses**   judges.

110–11 **instruction and amendment**   the play was originally performed at both universities and amended according to advice given.

111 **reduce**   restore.

113 **doctrine**   i.e. statement of beliefs.

115 **catastrophe**   dénouement, which is not strictly conventional as it is not 'happy' (i.e. Bonario and Celia cannot marry as she is already bound to Corvino).

121 **snaffle in their mouths**   gag them (Puritans).

127 **mulcted**   punished.

134–5 **worthier fruits**   better plays.

138 **primitive habit**   ancient status.

happiest monarchs. This it is, that hath not only rapt me   105
to present indignation, but made me studious heretofore,
and by all my actions to stand off from them; which may
most appear in this my latest work (which you, most
learned arbitresses, have seen, judged, and to my crown,
approved) wherein I have laboured, for their instruction   110
and amendment, to reduce not only the ancient forms, but
manners of the scene – the easiness, the propriety, the innocence, and last the doctrine, which is the principal end
of poesy: to inform men in the best reason of living. And
though my catastrophe may, in the strict rigour of comic   115
law,·meet with censure, as turning back to my promise, I
desire the learned and charitable critic to have so much
faith in me to think it was done of industry. For with what
ease I could have varied it nearer his scale (but that I fear
to boast my own faculty) I could here insert. But my   120
special aim being to put the snaffle in their mouths that
cry out, we never punish vice in our interludes, &c., I took
the more liberty – though not without some lines of example drawn even in the ancients themselves, the goings out
of whose comedies are not always joyful, but oft-times the   125
bawds, the servants, the rivals, yea, and the masters are
mulcted; and fitly, it being the office of a comic poet to
imitate justice and instruct to life, as well as purity of language, or stir up gentle affections. To which I shall take
the occasion elsewhere to speak. For the present (most re-   130
verenced sisters) as I have cared to be thankful for your
affections past, and here made the understanding acquainted with some ground of your favours, let me not
despair their continuance, to the maturing of some worthier fruits; wherein, if my muses be true to me, I shall raise   135
the despised head of poetry again, and stripping her out of
those rotten and base rags wherewith the times have
adulterated her form, restore her to her primitive habit,
feature and majesty, and render her worthy to be
embraced and kissed of all the great and master-spirits of   140

146   **genus irritabile**   (Latin) angry people (i.e. the true poets).

146-7   *spout ink*   denounce them in print so that the insults will outlast their own
lives.

148   *Cinnamus*   a surgeon-barber in Ancient Rome reputably able to remove
slaves' brands.

our world. As for the vile and slothful, who never affected
an act worthy of celebration, or are so inward with their
own vicious natures as they worthily fear her, and think it
a high point of policy to keep her in contempt with their
declamatory and windy invectives: she shall out of just   145
rage incite her servants (who are *genus irritabile*) to spout
ink in their faces that shall eat farther than their marrow,
into their fames; and not Cinnamus the barber with his art
shall be able to take out the brands, but they shall live and
be read till the wretches die, as things worst deserving of   150
themselves in chief, and then of all mankind.

   From my house in the Blackfriars this 11. of February. 1607   .

In order to appreciate Jonson's characterisation it is important to know the significance of the Italian names he used.

Volpone   fox.

Mosca   fly.

Voltore   vulture.

Corbaccio   raven.

Corvino   crow.

Bonario   derived from the word *buono* meaning 'good, untainted'.

Peregrine   falcon.

Sir Politic   often abbreviated to 'Pol' indicating a parrot.

CHARACTERS

in the play

VOLPONE, *a magnifico*
MOSCA, *his parasite*
VOLTORE, *an advocate*
CORBACCIO, *an old gentleman*
CORVINO, *a merchant*
BONARIO, *son of Corbaccio*
CELIA, *wife of Corvino*
SIR POLITIC WOULD-BE, *a knight*
PEREGRINE, *a gentleman traveller*
LADY WOULD-BE, *wife of Sir Politic*
NANO, *a dwarf*
CASTRONE, *a eunuch*
ANDROGYNO, *a hermaphrodite*
AVOCATORI, *four magistrates*
NOTARIO, *a notary*
MERCATORI, *three merchants*
COMMANDADORI, *officers*
SERVANTS
WAITING-WOMEN
A CROWD

The Scene:
VENICE

This is in the form of an acrostic, based around the name of the central character. It summarises the plot, telling of how Volpone lies supine, affecting illness, whilst his servant, Mosca, entices potential heirs to shower gifts upon him in the hope of guaranteeing their status in the old man's will.

2 **state** estate.

3 **languishing** apparently diminishing in strength.

 his parasite a servant who depends upon his master for his living.

5 **which ope themselves** which develop.

6 **when, bold** when confident.

7 **all are sold** all are betrayed.

This would be spoken by one of the cast to the audience and is a justification of the play. In it, Jonson praises his own skill as a dramatist whilst criticising those whose talents as comic writers go no further than the writing of crude slapstick.

3 **palates of the season** tastes of the time.

7 **hath been this measure** has been his aim.

9 **(whose throats ... failing)** who give themselves sore throats by their constant envious abuse.

10 **'All he writes, is railing'** all he is capable of writing is abuse.

12 **With saying, ... about them'** Jonson was criticised by his contemporaries for the slow speed at which he produced plays. In an age when writers tended to be prolific, he was noted for the care he took in re-drafting work.

13–15 **To these ... mend it** the answer to these is that the play did not exist two months ago and that it would take them five lifetimes to improve upon it.

17 **without a coadjutator** without a co-author – at this time it was common practice for writers to engage helpers.

18 **Novice, journeyman, or tutor** a 'novice' was an apprentice; a 'journeyman', a writer paid a daily wage to complete mundane passages; a 'tutor', one who proof-read the original.

20 **no eggs are broken** there is no crude slapstick in the play – again Jonson is jibing at his critics and lesser writers.

The Argument

V OLPONE, childless, rich, feigns sick, despairs,
O ffers his state to hopes of several heirs,
L ies languishing; his parasite receives
P resents of all, assures, deludes; then weaves
O ther cross-plots, which ope themselves, are told.   5
N ew tricks for safety are sought; they thrive; when, bold,
E ach tempts th'other again, and all are sold.

Prologue

Now, luck God sent us, and a little wit
   Will serve to make our play hit;
According to the palates of the season,
   Here is rhyme, not empty of reason:
This we were bid to credit from our poet,   5
   Whose true scope, if you would know it,
In all his poems still hath been this measure,
   To mix profit with your pleasure;
And not as some (whose throats their envy failing)
   Cry hoarsely, 'All he writes, is railing';   10
And, when his plays come forth, think they can flout them,
   With saying, 'He was a year about them.'
To these there needs no lie but this his creature,
   Which was, two months since, no feature;
And, though he dares give them five lives to mend it,   15
   'Tis known, five weeks fully penned it –
From his own hand, without a coadjutor,
Novice, journeyman, or tutor,
Yet, thus much I can give you, as a token
   Of his play's worth: no eggs are broken;   20

21 **Nor quaking ... affrighted**   again an attack upon slapstick – this could refer to a tradition at Lord Mayor's feasts where a huge custard was placed upon a table for jesters to jump into. It could also refer to stereotypical characterisations in what Jonson regarded as crude farces.

22 **rout**   the rabble (i.e. common play-goers).

23–4 **Nor hales ... writing**   nor does he drag in a fool to issue old proverbs and jokes in order to hide the mediocrity of the plot.

27 **for jests ... each table**   with jokes stolen from many sources.

33–4 **All gall ... remaineth**   gall and copperas were ingredients in ink. Both were associated with bitterness, the former because bad humour was attributed to the gall bladder, the latter because it was type of acid. Jonson says he has replaced both sources of bitterness in humour with salt, a cleansing agent. Therefore, the aim of his play is to cleanse human corruption, rather than just to insult.

Nor quaking custards with fierce teeth affrighted,
    Wherewith your rout are so delighted;
Nor hales he in a gull, old ends reciting,
    To stop gaps in his loose writing;
With such a deal of monstrous and forced action,   25
    As might make Bedlam a faction;
Nor made he his play for jests stol'n from each table,
    But makes jests to fit his fable.
And so presents quick comedy, refined
    As best critics have designed;   30
The laws of time, place, persons he observeth,
    From no needful rule he swerveth.
All gall and copperas from his ink he draineth,
    Only a little salt remaineth,
Wherewith he'll rub your cheeks, till, red with laughter,   35
    They shall look fresh a week after.

Summary of the plot

Act I

As the Act opens, we are introduced to the central character of the play, Volpone. He is feigning illness in order to take advantage of a custom (dating back to Ancient Greece) by which people gave rich men who were dying lavish gifts in order to secure a place as their heir; the principle was to invest a little now in order to reap a lot later.

Volpone expounds his love of gold to the audience: he believes that he who has it, has, 'virtue, fame, Honour, and all things else'. His chief boast is that he does not have to work to get rich, he can rely upon his natural cunning. At this point we are introduced to Mosca, his servant, a man who relies upon his intelligence and powers of flattery to secure his place in Volpone's household. The two make a formidable team.

The Act develops into a procession of potential suitors: Voltore, Corbaccio and Corvino. Each is fooled into giving Volpone riches; each leaves convinced that he is to be the heir of the dying man. Mosca works each as a puppeteer.

The Act ends with mention of Celia, the beautiful wife of Corvino. Volpone determines to see her.

Act 2

At this point, we step out of the claustrophobic setting of Volpone's chamber and into the wider environs of the city. In doing so, we quickly see that the same skewed moral values abound.

This Act sees the introduction of the sub-plot, the adventures of Sir Politic Would-be and his wife in Venice. The two are a satire of the English abroad but serve also to burlesque the actions of the major players. In this Act, the Sir Politic Would-be, a gullible fool, falls into company with Peregrine (Pilgrim-hawk), a fellow-traveller. The function of the latter is to highlight the folly of the former.

We also see Volpone, disguised as a mountebank, caught in the act of seducing Celia by the jealous Corvino. Once again, Mosca steps in, and soon convinces the legacy-hunter that it would be wise to offer his wife to his dying benefactor.

Act 3

The Act begins with Mosca singing the praise of nature's parasite, comparing his intelligence to that of lesser fools. He then accosts Bonario and tells him of his father's plan to disinherit him, taking him to Volpone's house for him to overhear the proof. His scheme is spoiled by the early arrival of Corvino and the unwilling Celia. In the scene which follows, Volpone's attempts at seduction fail and he resorts to force. Bonario intercedes and, having assaulted both master and servant, he and Celia flee to seek legal recourse.

It looks increasingly as if Volpone and Mosca have over-reached themselves and both fall into temporary despair. Has the fox been ensnared in a trap of his own making?

Act 4

After a brief farcical interlude with the Politic Would-bes, the action centres around the attempt by Bonario and Celia to get legal redress against Volpone. The major judges in Venice hear the case. Volpone's only hope lies in the hold his parasite exercises over the legacy-hunters. Will he be skilled enough to get them to place their greed above their reputations, and so pervert the course of justice?

Act 5

Volpone, triumphant, cannot resist another stratagem. It is announced that he is dead and the suitors come rushing to his house, only to find Mosca installed as heir. They leave dismayed, followed by the two conspirators in disguise. However, things do not go as planned and, as another crisis looms, Volpone and his parasite find themselves on opposite sides: pitted against each other, will they succeed where the forces of justice have failed, and bring about their own downfall?

1 · **Good morning**   the action of the play takes place within a single day.

2–26 **Open the shrine ... all things else**   the opening speech of the leading character is a eulogy to gold and, as such, is full of blasphemous references to its grandeur. It introduces the major theme of the play: greed. Venice will be seen as a world perverted by the lust for riches, a lust which will make men sell themselves and their families for the promise of future gain.

2 **shrine ... saint**   Volpone refers to his gold as a relic to be worshipped, a saint to be venerated.

3 **the world's soul**   Volpone is punning on the word *sol*, meaning sun – gold is the true reason why men rise in the morning.

5 **the horns of the celestial Ram**   this refers to the sign of the zodiac, Aries (March 21 – April 19), and the notion that it signifies the beginning of spring.

8–9 **or like ... Chaos**   to Volpone, his gold is like God's creation of light at the beginning of the world – it is the first and most important creation.

10 **son of Sol**   Sol was the god of the sun in mythology.

15 **Title ... the best**   the Golden Age of Greek and Roman mythology, a time of unequalled contentment.

16–18 **transcending ... on earth**   for Volpone, gold offers enjoyment far beyond that of human kinship.

19–20 **when they to ... Cupids**   when poets spoke of the beauty of the goddess of love as being 'golden' they should have given her twenty thousand sons not one. Again gold is linked with the notion of fertility – gold breeds gold, in Volpone's eyes.

22 **dumb god**   gold.

24–5 **The price ... heaven!**   Volpone here becomes more shocking, comparing the sacrifice of Christ for mankind to the purchasing power of gold. He goes on to say that hell would be as acceptable as heaven if one were allowed to keep one's gold in it.

Act One

Scene one

volpone's *House*
Enter volpone, mosca
volpone
Good morning to the day; and, next, my gold!
Open the shrine, that I may see my saint.
(mosca reveals the treasure)
Hail the world's soul, and mine! More glad than is
The teeming earth to see the longed-for sun
Peep through the horns of the celestial Ram,   5
Am I, to view thy splendour, darkening his;
That, lying here, amongst my other hoards,
Show'st like a flame by night; or like the day
Struck out of Chaos, when all darkness fled
Unto the centre. O, thou son of Sol   10
(But brighter than thy father) let me kiss,
With adoration, thee, and every relic
Of sacred treasure in this blessed room.
Well did wise poets by thy glorious name
Title that age which they would have the best,   15
Thou being the best of things – and far transcending
All style of joy, in children, parents, friends,
Or any other waking dream on earth.
Thy looks, when they to Venus did ascribe,
They should have given her twenty thousand Cupids;   20
Such are thy beauties, and our loves! Dear saint,
Riches, the dumb god that giv'st all men tongues;
That canst do naught, and yet mak'st men do all things;
The price of souls; even hell, with thee to boot,
Is made worth heaven! Thou art virtue, fame,   25
Honour, and all things else! Who can get thee,
He shall be noble, valiant, honest, wise –

28–9 **Riches are ... in nature**   Mosca shows himself to be like his master, preferring temporal riches to natural ones.

30–2 **Yet I glory ... possession**   these are key lines to understanding Volpone's character – it is not the possession of gold which enraptures him so much as the pursuit of it. He enjoys the chase more than the actual quarry.

34–5 **fat no beasts ... shambles**   Volpone boasts that he does not need to work to make money. He does not need to fatten livestock for the slaughterhouse.

36 **or men ... powder**   nor does he need to exploit workers until they die.

37 **subtle glass**   delicate glass, for which Venice was, and still is, famous.

38 **furrow-facèd**   image to describe the waves of an angry sea.

40 **usure private**   a common practice of the time: loaning out money at high interest rates. It was frowned upon by the Church.

40–7 **No sir ... is rotten**   Mosca supports Volpone's justification of his way of life. He denies that Volpone cons easy targets ('Soft prodigals') or cheats the young of their inheritance as usurers do, nor does he reclaim debts by having men thrown into prisons where they will die from the terrible conditions.

42–3 **your Dutch ... butter**   the Dutch were famous for their love of butter.

52–61 **And besides, sir ... soft beds**   Mosca goes on to praise Volpone's lavish use of his riches, contrasting his actions to the farmer who reaps a bumper harvest of corn yet eats only 'bitter herbs' or the merchant who has vaults of the finest wines but drinks only the cheapest (from Lombardy).

MOSCA

    And what he will, sir. Riches are in fortune
    A greater good than wisdom is in nature.

VOLPONE

    True, my beloved Mosca. Yet, I glory   30
    More in the cunning purchase of my wealth
    Than in the glad possession; since I gain
    No common way: I use no trade, no venture;
    I wound no earth with ploughshares; fat no beasts
    To feed the shambles; have no mills for iron,   35
    Oil, corn, or men, to grind 'em into powder;
    I blow no subtle glass; expose no ships
    To threat'nings of the furrow-facèd sea;
    I turn no moneys in the public bank;
    Nor usure private –

MOSCA   No sir, nor devour   40
    Soft prodigals. You shall ha' some will swallow
    A melting heir as glibly as your Dutch
    Will pills of butter, and ne'er purge for't;
    Tear forth the fathers of poor families
    Out of their beds, and coffin them, alive,   45
    In some kind, clasping prison, where their bones
    May be forth-coming when the flesh is rotten.
    But your sweet nature doth abhor these courses;
    You loathe, the widow's or the orphan's tears
    Should wash your pavements, or their piteous cries   50
    Ring in your roofs, and beat the air for vengeance –

VOLPONE

    Right, Mosca, I do loathe it.

MOSCA   And besides, sir,
    You are not like the thresher, that doth stand
    With a huge flail, watching a heap of corn,
    And, hungry, dares not taste the smallest grain,   55
    But feeds on mallows and such bitter herbs;
    Nor like the merchant, who hath filled his vaults
    With Romagnìa and rich Candian wines,

62–6 **You know ... maintenance**   Mosca now moves on to his true purpose: the flattery has been solely to acquire a tip for himself.

71 **cocker up my genius**   indulge my high spirits.

74–81 **but whom ... upon them**   an explanation to the audience of the purpose of the suitors soon to come.

82 **engross me**   inherit all of my wealth.

83 **counter-work**   plot against each other.

86 **And am content ... profit**   to exchange their hopes for my own profit.

88 **bearing them in hand**   leading them on.

89–90 **Letting the cherry ... again**   Volpone describes how he entices his suitors by letting them feel the prize then drawing it away. The reference is to a game called bob-cherry, in which cherries were dangled on strings for players to bite at without using their hands.

Yet drinks the lees of Lombard's vinegar;
You will not lie in straw, whilst moths and worms   60
Feed on your sumptuous hangings and soft beds.
You know the use of riches, and dare give, now,
From that bright heap, to me, your poor observer,
Or to your dwarf, or your hermaphrodite,
Your eunuch, or what other household trifle.   65
Your pleasure allows maintenance –

VOLPONE   Hold thee, Mosca,
                                        (*Gives him money*)
Take, of my hand; thou strik'st on truth in all,
And they are envious, term thee parasite.
Call forth my dwarf, my eunuch, and my fool,
And let 'em make me sport. (*Exit* MOSCA) What should I
    do   70
But cocker up my genius and live free
To all delights my fortune calls me to?
I have no wife, no parent, child, ally,
To give my substance to; but whom I make
Must be my heir – and this makes men observe me.   75
This draws new clients, daily, to my house,
Women and men, of every sex and age,
That bring me presents, send me plate, coin, jewels,
With hope that when I die (which they expect
Each greedy minute) it shall then return   80
Tenfold upon them; whilst some, covetous
Above the rest, seek to engross me, whole,
And counter-work the one unto the other,
Contend in gifts, as they would seem in love.
All which I suffer, playing with their hopes,   85
And am content to coin 'em into profit,
And look upon their kindness, and take more,
And look on that; still bearing them in hand,
Letting the cherry knock against their lips,
And draw it by their mouths, and back again. How
    now!   90

25

The opening is difficult for the modern audience and is frequently left out of productions. It is an entertainment devised by Mosca and performed by three of Volpone's household, the dwarf, the eunuch and the hermaphrodite. All are freaks, extreme forms of the human corruption which runs throughout the play. The entertainment is based around Pythagoras's belief that the human soul travels from one body to the next (transmigration of souls). It charts the journey of the soul which possessed Pythagoras's body, tracing its steady corruption as it moves towards modern times.

1 *room for fresh gamesters* make room for new actors.

3 *rehearse* recite.

4 *May not ... verse* may not be received badly because of its irregular verse. The piece is written as a parody of a morality play.

6–7 *Pythagoras ... divine* Pythagoras, a great mathematician and philosopher, is here presented as a fool.

8–21 *Apollo ... Crates the Cynic* the passage of the soul is traced from Apollo, son of Zeus and paragon of male beauty, to Aethalides, the son of Mercury who had the gift of an infallible memory, to Euphorbus, a warrior in the Trojan wars, and then to Meneleus, husband to the unfaithful Helen of Troy. Hermotimus and Pyrrhus, Greek philosophers, are next, then Pythagoras. Then the soul moves into Aspasia, the companion of the statesman Pericles, characteristically portrayed here as a whore, and then to another philosopher, Crates, who led a sect called the cynics.

22–48 *Since kings ... transmigration* the soul now enters a decline going from a king to a fool to a badger. This sets up a revelation of its forms in modern times, in which, continuing a downward spiral, it enters those Jonson most despised: a lawyer and, worst of all, a Puritan. From there, it can only become a hermaphrodite.

Scene two

Enter MOSCA, *with* NANO, ANDROGYNO, *and* CASTRONE, *ready to enter-tain* VOLPONE

NANO

Now, room for fresh gamesters, who do will you to know,
  They do bring you neither play nor university show;
And therefore do intreat you that whatsoever they rehearse
  May not fare a whit the worse for the false pace of the verse.
If you wonder at this, you will wonder more ere we pass,   5
  For know (*Pointing to* ANDROGYNO), here is enclosed the soul of Pythagoras,
That juggler divine, as hereafter shall follow;
  Which soul (fast and loose, sir) came first from Apollo,
And was breathed into Aethalides, Mercurius his son,
  Where it had the gift to remember all that ever was done.   10
From thence it fled forth, and made quick transmigration
  To goldy-locked Euphorbus, who was killed in good fashion
At the siege of old Troy, by the cuckold of Sparta.
  Hermotimus was next (I find it in my charta)
To whom it did pass, where no sooner it was missing.   15
  But with one Pyrrhus, of Delos, it learned to go a-fishing;
And thence did it enter the sophist of Greece.
  From Pythagore, she went into a beautiful piece
Hight Aspasia, the meretrix; and the next toss of her
  Was, again, of a whore – she became a philosopher,   20
Crates the Cynic (as itself does relate it).
  Since, kings, knights, and beggars, knaves, lords and fools gat it,

26 *Or his one ... Quater!'* refers to Pythagoras's theories of mathematics.

27 *His musics ... golden thigh* he is believed to be the discoverer of the numerical ratios determining the intervals on the musical scales and the laws concerning a right-angled triangle. He is also fabled to have had a golden thigh.

30 *shifted thy coat* changed your shape.

31–2 *Like one ... heresy* Johnson, a Catholic, denounces all who changed their beliefs with the Reformation.

34 *Carthusian* a religious order which could eat fish but not meat (unlike Pythagoras who forbade his followers both).

35 *dogmatical silence* followers of Pythagoras were instructed to obey a five-year silence.

36 *obstreperous lawyer* a loud-mouthed lawyer.

43 *By others ... brother* Jonson traces the soul's progress from a mule to its relation, a Puritan. The adjectives are terms Puritans used for themselves; the use of ass illustrates Jonson's opinion of them.

Besides ox, and ass, camel, mule, goat, and brock,
  In all which it hath spoke, as in the cobbler's cock.
But I come not here, to discourse of that matter,   25
  Or his one, two, or three, or his great oath, 'By
  Quater!'
His musics, his trigon, his golden thigh,
  Or his telling how elements shift; but I
Would ask, how of late thou hast suffered translation,
  And shifted thy coat in these days of reformation?   30

ANDROGYNO

Like one of the reformèd, a fool, as you see,
  Counting all old doctrine heresy.

NANO

But not on thine own forbid meats hast thou ventured?

ANDROGYNO

On fish, when first a Carthusian I entered.

NANO

Why, then thy dogmatical silence hath left thee?   35

ANDROGYNO

Of that an obstreperous lawyer bereft me.

NANO

O wonderful change! when Sir Lawyer forsook thee,
  For Pythagore's sake, what body then took thee?

ANDROGYNO

A good dull mule.

NANO   And how! by that means
  Thou wert brought to allow of the eating of beans?   40

ANDROGYNO

Yes.

NANO   But, from the mule, into whom did'st thou pass?

ANDROGYNO

Into a very strange beast, by some writers called an
  ass;
By others, a precise, pure, illuminate brother,
  Of those devour flesh, and sometimes one another;

46 **nativity-pie**   Christmas pie – renamed by Puritans to avoid the Popish associations of the suffix -*mas*.

47 **profane nation**   irreverent sect.

50 **an hermaphrodite**   known as a creature of pleasure because it possesses both male and female sexual organs.

55–8 **Alas ... most distressèd**   the soul, having experienced all human forms, chooses the most base rather than the grandest. The choice is not made because of the sexual possibilities of its current form but because it prefers decadence and stupidity to the sacrifice and hardship expected of the great – an indication of the corrupted values at the heart of Venetian society.

And will drop you forth a libel, or a sanctified lie,   45
   Betwixt every spoonful of a nativity-pie.

NANO

   Now quit thee, for heaven, of that profane nation;
    And gently report thy next transmigration.

ANDROGYNO

   To the same that I am.

NANO   A creature of delight?

   And, what is more than a fool, an hermaphrodite?   50
   Now pray thee, sweet soul, in all thy variation,
    Which body would'st thou choose, to take up thy
    station?

ANDROGYNO

   Troth, this I am in, even here would I tarry.

NANO

   'Cause here the delight of each sex thou canst vary?

ANDROGYNO

   Alas, those pleasures be stale and forsaken;   55
    No, 'tis your fool, wherewith I am so taken;
   The only one creature that I can call blessèd,
    For all other forms I have proved most distressèd.

NANO

   Spoke true, as thou wert in Pythagoras still.
    This learned opinion we celebrate will,   60
   Fellow eunuch, as behoves us, with all our wit and art,
   To dignify that whereof ourselves are so great and
    special a part.

VOLPONE

   Now very, very pretty! Mosca, this
   Was thy invention?

MOSCA   If it please my patron,
   Not else.

VOLPONE   It doth, good Mosca.

MOSCA   Then it was, sir.   65

67–82 **Song**   this is a celebration of the role of the fool, popular with all because he can speak the truth without being punished. The ladies particularly like him because what he lacks in brains he has been compensated for in sexual potency. Thus his merits are his 'Tongue' (wit) and 'bauble' (penis).

84 **Signior Voltore, the advocate**   one of Volpone's principal suitors is a lawyer, aptly named Voltore (vulture) (see note to characters' names, page 12).

85–6 **Fetch me ... night caps**   Volpone quickly assumes the garb of the invalid. Fittingly, when dealing with his 'heirs' he dons the fur of the fox.

89–90 **vulture ... gor-crow**   Volpone has no doubts about the motives of his visitors, picturing them as birds of prey waiting to pick at his corpse. He lists the vulture (Voltore), the kite (Lady Would-be), the raven (Corbaccio) and the carrion crow (Corvino).

Song

Fools, they are the only nation
Worth men's envy or admiration;
Free from care or sorrow-taking,
Selves and others merry making.   70
All they speak, or do, is sterling:
Your fool, he is your great man's darling,
And your ladies' sport and pleasure;
Tongue and bauble are his treasure.
E'en his face begetteth laughter,   75
And he speaks truth, free from slaughter;
He's the grace of every feast,
And sometimes the chiefest guest;
Hath his trencher and his stool,
When wit waits upon the fool.   80
   O, who would not be
   Hee, hee, hee?

One knocks without

VOLPONE
Who's that? Away!

(*Exeunt* NANO, CASTRONE)

Look Mosca!

MOSCA   Fool, begone!

Exit ANDROGYNO

'Tis Signior Voltore, the advocate;
I know him by his knock.

VOLPONE   Fetch me my gown,   85
My furs, and night caps; say my couch is changing;
And let him entertain himself awhile
Without i' th' gallery. (*Exit* MOSCA) Now, now, my
   clients
Begin their visitation! vulture, kite,
Raven, and gor-crow, all my birds of prey,   90

33

94 **Massy, and antique**   heavy and old.

95–7 **and not a fox ... crow?**   this refers to Aesop's fable whereby a fox tricked a crow into dropping a piece of cheese it was carrying by praising its singing voice.

102 **That this would fetch you**   that this would persuade you.

108 **as lettered as himself**   Mosca believes Voltore's delusions show that his horse is as learned as he is.

111–14 **O, no ... cathedral doctor**   Mosca and Volpone both appreciate that, in Venice, to be rich is to be highly valued, regardless of one's personal qualities. Thus an ass can be accepted as a wise man if its clothing is fine enough. It is this hypocrisy which the two set out to exploit so successfully.

That think me turning carcass, now they come –
I am not for 'em yet. How now? the news?

Re-enter MOSCA

MOSCA

A piece of plate, sir.

VOLPONE   Of what bigness?

MOSCA   Huge,
Massy, and antique, with your name inscribed,
And arms engraven.

VOLPONE   Good! and not a fox   95
Stretched on the earth, with fine delusive sleights,
Mocking a gaping crow? ha, Mosca?

MOSCA   Sharp, sir.

VOLPONE

Give me my furs. Why dost thou laugh so, man?

MOSCA

I cannot choose, sir, when I apprehend
What thoughts he has, without, now, as he walks: 100
That this might be the last gift he should give;
That this would fetch you; if you died today
And gave him all, what he should be tomorrow;
What large return would come of all his ventures;
How he should worshipped be, and reverenced;   105
Ride, with his furs, and foot-cloths; waited on
By herds of fools and clients; have clear way
Made for his mule, as lettered as himself;
Be called the great and learned advocate;
And then concludes, there's naught impossible.   110

VOLPONE

Yes, to be learned, Mosca.

MOSCA   O, no – rich
Implies it. Hood an ass with reverend purple,
So you can hide his two ambitious ears,
And he shall pass for a cathedral doctor.

VOLPONE

My caps, my caps, good Mosca. Fetch him in.   115

119–23 **Thanks ... Loving Mosca!** this exchange shows the true nature of their relationship. Mosca flatters extravagantly to keep himself in favour; Volpone recognises this but is pleased nonetheless and encourages it when he has time to listen. Despite their words of affection, theirs is a false friendship.

123 **harpies** mythical monsters which were half-bird and half-human. As such, they were grasping – thus the image of the legacy-hunters is sustained.

125–9 **Now my feigned ... O!** in his list of ailments, his preparation and subsequent performance, Volpone shows himself the consummate actor, revelling in his role.

125 **phthisic** consumption; tuberculosis.

126 **apoplexy** fits of unconsciousness.

1 **what you were, sir** i.e. the most favoured of the legacy-hunters.

5 **good meaning to** your good intentions to him.

6 **come most grateful** cannot be but welcome.

MOSCA

Stay, sir, your ointment for your eyes.

VOLPONE   That's true;

Dispatch, dispatch – I long to have possession

Of my new present.

MOSCA   That, and thousands more,

I hope to see you lord of.

VOLPONE   Thanks, kind Mosca.

MOSCA

And that, when I am lost in blended dust,   120

And hundred such as I am, in succession –

VOLPONE

Nay, that were too much, Mosca.

MOSCA   You shall live,

Still, to delude these harpies.

VOLPONE   Loving Mosca!

'Tis well. My pillow now, and let him enter.

                                        (*Exit* MOSCA)

Now, my feigned cough, my phthisic, and my gout,   125

My apoplexy, palsy, and catarrhs,

Help, with your forced functions, this my posture,

Wherein, this three year, I have milked their hopes.

He comes, I hear him – uh! uh! uh! uh! O –

Scene three

Enter MOSCA, *with* VOLTORE *bearing a piece of plate*

MOSCA

You still are what you were, sir. Only you –

Of all the rest – are he, commands his love;

And you do wisely to preserve it thus,

With early visitation, and kind notes

Of your good meaning to him, which, I know,   5

Cannot but come most grateful. Patron, sir.

Here's Signior Voltore is come –

10 **bought of St Mark** purchased from a goldsmith's in St Mark's Square, an area renowned for such dealing.

12 **Pray ... more often** in this exchange, as in so many others, we see Volpone's enjoyment of his scheming. The line is encouraging to Voltore, as it seems to confirm him as a favourite; its real meaning is that Volpone likes him to come often because he brings gifts.

15 **The plate is here** feigning deafness and now blindness, Volpone reaches out to touch Voltore's hand. Mosca cannot resist indicating what Volpone really wants to get hold of.

18 **That he is not weaker** Mosca interprets Voltore's real meaning in an aside.

19 **munificent** generous.

19–20 **No, sir ... plate** if only I could give you health as easily as the plate. Notice how here, speech either has a double meaning or smells of hypocrisy.

21–2 **Your love ... taste in this** your love is revealed in this gift.

VOLPONE   What say you?

MOSCA

Sir, Signior Voltore is come this morning
To visit you.

VOLPONE   I thank him.

MOSCA   And hath brought
A piece of antique plate, bought of St Mark,   10
With which he here presents you.

VOLPONE   He is welcome.
Pray him to come more often.

MOSCA   Yes.

VOLTORE   What says he?

MOSCA

He thanks you, and desires you see him often.

VOLPONE

Mosca!

MOSCA   My patron?

VOLPONE   Bring him near, where is he?
I long to feel his hand.

MOSCA   The plate is here, sir.   15

VOLTORE

How fare you, sir?

VOLPONE   I thank you, Signior Voltore.
Where is the plate? Mine eyes are bad.

VOLTORE   I'm sorry
To see you still thus weak.

MOSCA (*Aside*)   That he is not weaker.

VOLPONE

You are too munificent.

VOLTORE   No, sir, would to heaven
I could as well give health to you as that plate.   20

VOLPONE

You give, sir, what you can. I thank you. Your love
Hath taste in this, and shall not be unanswered.
I pray you see me often.

VOLTORE   Yes, I shall, sir.

29 **I am sailing to my port**   Volpone feigns death, using a suitably awful euphemism, in order to whet his suitor's appetite a little more; to increase the torture when he does not die.

34–5 **you will vouchsafe ... family**   Mosca adds to the realism by begging to be taken into Voltore's household when Volpone dies.

37 **the rising sun**   i.e. Voltore. Mosca continues to pretend to flatter him as if he was the new master.

39–40 **have not done ... offices**   have not done you any bad services.

40–44 **hear I wear ... goods here**   Mosca continues to lead Voltore on by describing all of Volpone's goods as 'your'.

VOLPONE

Be not far from me.

MOSCA (*Aside to* VOLTORE) Do you observe that, sir?

VOLPONE

Hearken unto me still. It will concern you.   25

MOSCA

You are a happy man, sir; know your good.

VOLPONE

I cannot now last long –

MOSCA (*Aside to* VOLTORE) You are his heir, sir.

VOLTORE

Am I?

VOLPONE I feel me going – uh! uh! uh! uh! –

I am sailing to my port – uh! uh! uh! uh! –

And I am glad I am so near my haven.   30

MOSCA

Alas, kind gentleman; well, we must all go –

VOLTORE

But, Mosca –

MOSCA   Age will conquer.

VOLTORE   Pray thee hear me.

Am I inscribed his heir for certain?

MOSCA   Are you?

I do beseech you, sir, you will vouchsafe

To write me i' your family. All my hopes   35

Depend upon your worship. I am lost,

Except the rising sun do shine on me.

VOLTORE

It shall both shine and warm thee, Mosca.

MOSCA   Sir,

I am a man that have not done your love

All the worst offices; here I wear your keys,   40

See all your coffers and your caskets locked,

Keep the poor inventory of your jewels,

Your plate, and moneys; am your steward, sir,

Husband your goods here.

41

46 ***The wax is warm yet***   i.e. having just been sealed.

49 ***I know no second cause***   i.e. I know of no other cause for your success (he is inviting praise).

49–50 ***Thy modesty ... requite it***   Voltore has fallen for the act, promising to reward Mosca's good services.

51–66 ***He ever liked ... chequeen!***   in the speech which follows, Mosca pretends to admire the work of lawyers. In it, he actually reveals their hypocrisy, greed and immorality.

51 ***your course***   your profession.

58–9 ***Give forkèd .... put it up***   to give ambiguous advice, taking bribes from both sides and pocketing them without scruple.

63 ***so perplexed a tongue***   such bewildering speech.

64–5 ***that would not wag ... fee***   that will not even gossip, nor stay silent, without being paid to do so. Mosca is showing that a lawyer's mouth is always for hire, even if it is simply to keep it quiet.

66 ***a chequeen***   a gold coin.

70–2 ***When you ..... of the flood***   Mosca equates wealth with excess and, whilst Voltore will be enraptured by the images given, they are calculated to arouse disgust in a more discerning audience.

VOLTORE   But am I sole heir?

MOSCA

Without a partner, sir, confirmed this morning;   45
The wax is warm yet, and the ink scarce dry
Upon the parchment.

VOLTORE   Happy, happy, me!
By what good chance, sweet Mosca?

MOSCA   Your desert, sir;
I know no second cause.

VOLTORE   Thy modesty
Is loath to know it; well, we shall requite it.   50

MOSCA

He ever liked your course, sir – that first took him.
I oft have heard him say how he admired
Men of your large profession, that could speak
To every cause, and things mere contraries,
Till they were hoarse again, yet all be law;   55
That, with most quick agility, could turn,
And re-turn; make knots, and undo them;
Give forkèd counsel; take provoking gold
On either hand, and put it up – these men,
He knew, would thrive, with their humility.   60
And, for his part, he thought he should be blest
To have his heir of such a suffering spirit,
So wise, so grave, of so perplexed a tongue,
And loud withal, that would not wag, nor scarce
Lie still, without a fee; when every word   65
Your worship but lets fall, is a chequeen!

                                        (*Another knocks*)

Who's that? one knocks; I would not have you seen, sir.
And yet – pretend you came and went in haste;
I'll fashion an excuse. And, gentle sir,
When you do come to swim in golden lard,   70
Up to the arms in honey, that your chin
Is borne up stiff with fatness of the flood,
Think on your vassal; but remember me:

78 **Put business in your face**   make yourself look business-like.

2 **Stand there, and multiply**   Mosca means that the pile of gifts will increase with each caller.

3–4 **A wretch .... feign to be**   the next caller is Corbaccio, a man so old and frail that his role as a legacy-hunter is ludicrous. As Mosca says, he is closer to death than Volpone could ever pretend to be.

7 **What? mends he?**   Corbaccio's deafness is a source of humour throughout the play.

8 **That's well**   Corbaccio makes no pretence to Mosca about wanting Volpone dead.

I ha' not been your worst of clients.

VOLTORE   Mosca –

MOSCA

When will you have your inventory brought, sir?   75
Or see a copy of the will? (*Knocking again*) Anon!
I'll bring 'em to you, sir. Away, be gone;
Put business in your face.

Exit VOLTORE

VOLPONE   Excellent, Mosca!
Come hither, let me kiss thee.

MOSCA   Keep you still, sir.
Here is Corbaccio.

VOLPONE   Set the plate away.   80
The vulture's gone, and the old raven's come.

Scene four

MOSCA

Betake you to your silence, and your sleep.
(*To the plate*) Stand there, and multiply. Now shall we
    see
A wretch who is indeed more impotent
Than this can feign to be; yet hopes to hop
Over his grave. (*Enter* CORBACCIO) Signior Corbaccio!   5
You're very welcome, sir.

CORBACCIO   How does your patron?

MOSCA

Troth, as he did, sir, no amends.

CORBACCIO   What? mends he?

MOSCA

No, sir – he is rather worse.

CORBACCIO   That's well. Where is he?

MOSCA

Upon his couch, sir, newly fall'n asleep.

13   **An opiate**   a sedative.

14–18   **Why? I myself . . . take it**   Corbaccio's over-insistence on the purpose and purity of the draft makes Volpone believe it is poisoned.

20–4   **He has no . . . his heir**   Mosca, having attacked lawyers, now satirises doctors.

27   **they flay**   they strip a man (i.e. of money).

29   **And then, they . . . experiment**   they kill patients by testing new drugs on them.

CORBACCIO

    Does he sleep well?

MOSCA   No wink, sir, all this night,   10

    Nor yesterday, but slumbers.

CORBACCIO   Good! He should take

    Some counsel of physicians; I have brought him

    An opiate here, from mine own doctor –

MOSCA

    He will not hear of drugs.

CORBACCIO   Why? I myself

    Stood by while 't was made, saw all th'ingredients,   15

    And know it cannot but most gently work.

    My life for his, 'tis but to make him sleep.

VOLPONE (*Aside*)

    Ay, his last sleep, if he would take it.

MOSCA   Sir,

    He has no faith in physic.

CORBACCIO   Say you, say you?

MOSCA

    He has no faith in physic: he does think   20

    Most of your doctors are the greater danger,

    And worse disease t'escape. I often have

    Heard him protest that your physician

    Should never be his heir.

CORBACCIO   Not I his heir?

MOSCA

    Not your physician, sir.

CORBACCIO   O, no, no, no,   25

    I do not mean it.

MOSCA   No, sir, nor their fees

    He cannot brook; he says, they flay a man

    Before they kill him.

CORBACCIO   Right, I do conceive you.

MOSCA

    And then, they do it by experiment;

    For which the law not only doth absolve 'em,   30

32 **To hire**   to pay for.

45 **Good symptoms still**   i.e. they sound fatal.

48 **with a continual rheum**   constant stream of mucus from the eyes.

But gives them great reward; and he is loath
To hire his death so.

CORBACCIO   It is true, they kill
With as much licence as a judge.

MOSCA   Nay, more;
For he but kills, sir, where the law condemns,
And these can kill him, too.

CORBACCIO   Ay, or me –   35
Or any man. How does his apoplex?
Is that strong on him still?

MOSCA   Most violent.
His speech is broken, and his eyes are set.
His face drawn longer than 't was wont –

CORBACCIO   How? How?
Stronger than he was wont?

MOSCA   No, sir; his face   40
Drawn longer, than 't was wont.

CORBACCIO   O, good.

MOSCA   His mouth
Is ever gaping, and his eyelids hang.

CORBACCIO   Good.

MOSCA
A freezing numbness stiffens all his joints,
And makes the colour of his flesh like lead.

CORBACCIO   'Tis good.

MOSCA
His pulse beats slow, and dull.

CORBACCIO   Good symptoms still.   45

MOSCA
And, from his brain –

CORBACCIO   Ha? How? Not from his brain?

MOSCA
Yes, sir, and from his brain –

CORBACCIO   I conceive you, good.

MOSCA
Flows a cold sweat, with a continual rheum,

52 *scotomy* a dizziness, a temporary loss of understanding.

67 *By your own scale, sir* again, in an aside, Mosca criticises the suitors. He means Corbaccio can judge Voltore's unscrupulousness because it is a mirror of his own.

Forth the resolvèd corners of his eyes.
CORBACCIO
  Is't possible? Yet I am better, ha!   50
  How does he, with the swimming of his head?
MOSCA
  O, sir, 'tis past the scotomy; he now
  Hath lost his feeling, and hath left to snort;
  You hardly can perceive him, that he breathes.
CORBACCIO
  Excellent, excellent, sure I shall outlast him;   55
  This makes me young again, a score of years.
MOSCA
  I was a-coming for you, sir.
CORBACCIO   Has he made his will?
  What has he given me?
MOSCA   No, sir.
CORBACCIO   Nothing? ha?
MOSCA
  He has not made his will, sir.
CORBACCIO   Oh, oh, oh.
  What then did Voltore, the lawyer, here?   60
MOSCA
  He smelt a carcass, sir, when he but heard
  My master was about his testament –
  As I did urge him to it, for your good –
CORBACCIO
  He came unto him, did he? I thought so.
MOSCA
  Yes, and presented him this piece of plate.   65
CORBACCIO
  To be his heir?
MOSCA   I do not know, sir.
CORBACCIO   True,
  I know it too.
MOSCA (*Aside*) By your own scale, sir.
CORBACCIO   Well,

70 **weigh down**   outvalue.

73 **'Tis aurum ... potabile**   (Latin) it can be touched if not drunk (like medicine).

74 **It shall ... his bowl?**   Mosca picks up on the medicinal allusion by suggesting he put the gold in Volpone's dinner bowl.

80–1 **'Tis true ... me't again**   Mosca has made an error by suggesting that the gold may revive Volpone. Corbaccio immediately demands its return and the parasite must react quickly to avoid this.

I shall prevent him yet. See, Mosca, look,
Here, I have brought a bag of bright chequeens,
Will quite weigh down his plate.

MOSCA   Yea, marry, sir!   70
This is true physic, this your sacred medicine,
No talk of opiates, to this great elixir.

CORBACCIO
'Tis *aurum palpabile*, if not *potabile*.

MOSCA
It shall be ministered to him, in his bowl?

CORBACCIO
Ay, do, do, do.

MOSCA   Most blessed cordial!   75
This will recover him.

CORBACCIO   Yes, do, do, do.

MOSCA
I think it were not best, sir.

CORBACCIO   What?

MOSCA   To recover him.

CORBACCIO
O, no, no, no; by no means.

MOSCA   Why, sir, this
Will work some strange effect if he but feel it.

CORBACCIO
'Tis true, therefore forbear, I'll take my venture;   80
Give me't again.

MOSCA   At no hand, pardon me;
You shall not do yourself that wrong, sir. I
Will so advise you, you shall have it all.

CORBACCIO
How?

MOSCA All, sir, 'tis your right, your own; no man
Can claim a part; 'tis yours, without a rival,   85
Decreed by destiny.

CORBACCIO   How? how, good Mosca?

89 **re-importune** to beg again.

93–8 **Now, would I ... unto me** Mosca, aware Corbaccio could die at any time, now moves to secure his whole fortune for Volpone. He must convince the old man that he is disinheriting his son in appearance ('colour') only, as Volpone will die first: by this arrangement he will be able to make his son heir to a larger fortune.

104 **A son so ... meriting** Bonario will live up to this praise – he is a rare example of virtue in the play.

MOSCA

    I'll tell you, sir. This fit he shall recover –

CORBACCIO

    I do conceive you.

MOSCA   And, on first advantage

    Of his gained sense, will I re-importune him

    Unto the making of his testament,   90

    And show him this.

CORBACCIO   Good, good.

MOSCA   'Tis better yet,

    If you will hear, sir.

CORBACCIO   Yes, with all my heart.

MOSCA

    Now, would I counsel you, make home with speed;

    There, frame a will, whereto you shall inscribe

    My master your sole heir.

CORBACCIO   And disinherit   95

    My son?

MOSCA   O, sir, the better – for that colour

    Shall make it much more taking.

CORBACCIO   O, but colour?

MOSCA

    This will, sir, you shall send it unto me.

    Now, when I come to enforce (as I will do)

    Your cares, your watchings, and your many prayers,   100

    Your more than many gifts, your this day's present,

    And, last, produce your will; where (without thought

    Or least regard unto your proper issue,

    A son so brave and highly meriting)

    The stream of your diverted love hath thrown you   105

    Upon my master, and made him your heir.

    He cannot be so stupid, or stone dead,

    But, out of conscience, and mere gratitude –

CORBACCIO

    He must pronounce me his?

MOSCA   'Tis true.

109–10 **This plot ... on before**   Corbaccio claims the plot was an idea of his own. This shows his hypocrisy and also his stupidity: he has been hooked.

114 **Being so lusty**   being so healthy. Anyone but a fool would see the ridicule in this compliment – for Mosca and Volpone, the pleasure of the chase lies in its danger as well as the potential rewards.

116 **very organ**   i.e. an echo of my thoughts.

CORBACCIO   This plot
  Did I think on before.
MOSCA   I do believe it.   110
CORBACCIO
  Do you not believe it?
MOSCA   Yes, sir.
CORBACCIO   Mine own project.
MOSCA
  Which when he hath done, sir –
CORBACCIO   Published me his heir?
MOSCA
  And you so certain to survive him –
CORBACCIO   Ay.
MOSCA
  Being so lusty a man –
CORBACCIO   'Tis true.
MOSCA   Yes, sir –
CORBACCIO
  I thought on that too. See, how he should be   115
  The very organ to express my thoughts!
MOSCA
  You have not only done yourself a good –
CORBACCIO
  But multiplied it on my son?
MOSCA   'Tis right, sir.
CORBACCIO
  Still my invention.
MOSCA   'Las, sir, heaven knows,
  It hath been all my study, all my care,   120
  (I e'en grow grey withal) how to work things –
CORBACCIO
  I do conceive, sweet Mosca.
MOSCA   You are he
  For whom I labour here.
CORBACCIO   Ay, do, do, do.

124 **Rook go with you, raven**   may you be fooled.

125 **You do lie, sir**   Mosca, taking advantage of Corbaccio's deafness, becomes more bold in his insults.

128 **Nor I, to gull ... blessing**   Mosca picks up on the old man's intentions and, blasphemously declares that he would use his position to disinherit his new brother Bonario, much as Jacob did to Esau in Genesis. Once again, Corbaccio is oblivious.

141 **Pour oil into their ears**   i.e. flatter them.

I'll straight about it.

MOSCA (*Quietly*)   Rook go with you, raven.

CORBACCIO

I know thee honest.

MOSCA   You do lie, sir.

CORBACCIO   And –   125

MOSCA

Your knowledge is no better than your ears, sir.

CORBACCIO

I do not doubt to be a father to thee.

MOSCA

Nor I, to gull my brother of his blessing.

CORBACCIO

I may ha' my youth restored to me, why not?

MOSCA

Your worship is a precious ass –

CORBACCIO   What say'st thou?   130

MOSCA   .

I do desire your worship to make haste, sir.

CORBACCIO

'Tis done, 'tis done, I go

                                        Exit CORBACCIO

VOLPONE   O I shall burst;

Let out my sides, let out my sides –

MOSCA   Contain

Your flux of laughter, sir – you know this hope

Is such a bait, it covers any hook.   135

VOLPONE

O, but thy working, and thy placing it!

I cannot hold; good rascal, let me kiss thee –

I never knew thee in so rare a humour.

MOSCA

Alas, sir, I but do as I am taught;

Follow your grave instructions; give 'em words;   140

Pour oil into their ears; and send them hence.

142–3 **What a rare ... itself!**   Volpone mimics the moral, but it is one which will be vindicated at the end of the play: the joke will backfire on him.

156 **like Aeson**   father of Jason, his youth was restored by Medea.

159 **And all turns air!**   all turns into delusion.

161 **spruce**   trim and smart.

VOLPONE

    'Tis true, 'tis true. What a rare punishment
    Is avarice to itself!

MOSCA   Ay, with our help, sir.

VOLPONE

    So many cares, so many maladies,
    So many fears attending on old age,   145
    Yea, death so often called on, as no wish
    Can be more frequent with 'em. Their limbs faint,
    Their senses dull, their seeing, hearing, going,
    All dead before them; yea, their very teeth,
    Their instruments of eating, failing them –   150
    Yet this is reckoned life! Nay, here was one,
    Is now gone home, that wishes to live longer!
    Feels not his gout, nor palsy, feigns himself
    Younger, by scores of years, flatters his age
    With confident belying it, hopes he may   155
    With charms, like Aeson, have his youth restored;
    And with these thoughts so battens, as if fate
    Would be as easily cheated on as he,
    And all turns air!

                                    (Another knocks)

        Who's that, there, now? a third?

MOSCA

    Close, to your couch again; I hear his voice.   160
    It is Corvino, our spruce merchant.

VOLPONE *(Lying down)*   Dead.

MOSCA

    Another bout, sir, with your eyes. *(Applying more ointment)*

                    Who's there?

5 **How shall I do, then?**   how shall I make him aware of my gift? Again, we see that the concern of the legacy-hunter is not for Volpone's welfare but for his own.

9 **Is your pearl orient, sir?**   i.e. is it of the best quality?

14 **it doubles the twelfth carat**   i.e. it weighs twenty-four carats, and is thus very valuable.

Scene five

Enter CORVINO

MOSCA

    Signior Corvino! come most wished for! O,
    How happy were you, if you knew it, now!

CORVINO

    Why? what? wherein?

MOSCA   The tardy hour is come, sir.

CORVINO

    He is not dead?

MOSCA   Not dead, sir, but as good;
    He knows no man.

CORVINO   How shall I do, then?

MOSCA   Why, sir?   5

CORVINO

    I have brought him, here, a pearl.

MOSCA   Perhaps he has
    So much remembrance left, as to know you, sir;
    He still calls on you; nothing but your name
    Is in his mouth. Is your pearl orient, sir?

CORVINO

    Venice was never owner of the like.   10

VOLPONE (*Faintly*)

    Signior Corvino.

MOSCA   Hark.

VOLPONE   Signior Corvino.

MOSCA

    He calls you, step and give it him. He's here, sir.
    And he has brought you a rich pearl.

CORVINO   How do you, sir?
    Tell him, it doubles the twelfth carat.

MOSCA   Sir,
    He cannot understand, his hearing's gone;   15
    And yet it comforts him to see you –

CORVINO   Say

20 **See, how he grasps it!** Mosca intends Corvino to see Volpone as being
aware of the gift given, in order that he will continue to bring them. He is
also indulging himself, by laughing at how the supposedly feeble man is
suddenly vigorous at the sight of loot.

22–3 **The weeping ... visor** i.e. the sorrow of an heir at the death of his
benefactor should serve only to mask his glee at the fortune he has
inherited. Mosca once again confronts the suitors with the reality of their
feelings – he cuts through their mask of concern.

28 **gaping** Mosca intentionally uses this word as a reminder of the fable of the
crow and the fox. He constantly amuses himself at the legacy-hunters'
stupidity. He is also, of course, criticising Corvino but the latter is blind to
this.

37 **Nothing bequeathed ... curse** nothing has been left to them but the
opportunity to curse their luck at being unsuccessful.

39 **No more than a blind harper** this refers to an old proverb whereby harpers
were supposed to be blind

42–3 **Not those ... remember** Mosca is leading Corvone on with a description of
Volpone's comatose state. However, as with Corbaccio, he again goes too
far with his embellishments and panics his victim, this time with talk of
offspring. He reacts quickly by saying they are bastards and therefore have
no claim to an inheritance.

I have a diamond for him, too.

MOSCA   Best show't, sir,
Put it into his hand; 'tis only there
He apprehends – he has his feeling yet.
See, how he grasps it!

CORVINO   'Las, good gentleman!   20
How pitiful the sight is!

MOSCA   Tut, forget, sir.
The weeping of an heir should still be laughter
Under a visor.

CORVINO   Why, am I his heir?

MOSCA

Sir, I am sworn, I may not show the will
Till he be dead. But here has been Corbaccio,   25
Here has been Voltore, here were others too,
I cannot number 'em, they were so many,
All gaping here for legacies; but I,
Taking the vantage of his naming you,
'Signior Corvino, Signior Corvino', took   30
Paper, and pen, and ink, and there I asked him,
Whom he would have his heir? 'Corvino'. Who
Should be executor? 'Corvino'. And
To any question he was silent to,
I still interpreted the nods he made   35
Through weakness, for consent; and sent home
    th'others,
Nothing bequeathed them but to cry, and curse.

They embrace

CORVINO

O, my dear Mosca. Does he not perceive us?

MOSCA

No more than a blind harper. He knows no man,
No face of friend, nor name of any servant,   40
Who 'twas that fed him last, or gave him drink;
Not those he hath begotten or brought up
Can he remember.

47 **The dwarf ... his** this explains the presence of the freaks in the house. They are fitting offspring for Volpone, externalising his inner corruption.

51 **credit your own sense** trust your own eyes.

54–5 **For your incontinence ... throughly** you have been so lecherous that you deserve to have syphilis too. At this time this strain of venereal disease was fatal.

57–60 **Those filthy ... on end** the virulence of the verse here is such that one is left wondering whether Mosca is acting or whether he is venting his own spleen at his master.

60 **frozen dish-clouts** Mosca compares Volpone's cheeks to frozen rags, stiff and icy.

63 **a culverin** a long cannon.

66 **A very draught** a cesspool.

CORVINO   Has he children?
MOSCA   Bastards,
    Some dozen, or more, that he begot on beggars,
    Gipsies and Jews, and black-moors, when he was drunk.   45
    Knew you not that, sir? 'Tis the common fable.
    The dwarf, the fool, the eunuch are all his;
    He's the true father of his family,
    In all save me – but he has given 'em nothing.
CORVINO
    That's well, that's well. Art sure he does not hear us?   50
MOSCA
    Sure, sir? Why, look you, credit your own sense.
                              (*Shouts in* VOLPONE's *ear*)
    The pox approach and add to your diseases,
    If it would send you hence the sooner, sir.
    For your incontinence, it hath deserved it
    Throughly, and throughly, and the plague to boot.   55
    – (*To* CORVINO) You may come near, sir. – Would you
       once close
    Those filthy eyes of yours, that flow with slime
    Like two frog-pits; and those same hanging cheeks,
    Covered with hide instead of skin – Nay, help, sir –
    That look like frozen dish-clouts, set on end.   60
CORVINO
    Or, like an old smoked wall, on which the rain
    Ran down in streaks.
MOSCA   Excellent, sir, speak out;
    You may be louder yet; a culverin
    Dischargèd in his ear would hardly bore it.
CORVINO
    His nose is like a common sewer, still running.   65
MOSCA
    'Tis good! And what his mouth?
CORVINO   A very draught.
MOSCA
    O, stop it up –

74 **Nay, at your discretion** Mosca taunts Corvino by suggesting they murder Volpone. The suitor is not averse to the idea but is terrified of being involved and prepares to leave.

82 **Your gallant wife** the mention of his wife sets the jealous Corvino scuttling off.

CORVINO   By no means.
MOSCA   Pray you, let me.
Faith, I would stifle him rarely with a pillow,
As well as any woman that should keep him.
CORVINO
Do as you will, but I'll be gone.
MOSCA   Be so;   70
It is your presence makes him last so long.
CORVINO
I pray you, use no violence.
MOSCA   No, sir? why?
Why should you be thus scrupulous, pray you, sir?
CORVINO
Nay, at your discretion.
MOSCA   Well, good sir, be gone.
CORVINO
I will not trouble him now, to take my pearl?   75
MOSCA
Puh! nor your diamond. What a needless care
Is this afflicts you! Is not all here yours?
Am not I here? whom you have made? your creature?
That owe my being to you?
CORVINO   Grateful Mosca!
Thou art my friend, my fellow, my companion,   80
My partner, and shalt share in all my fortunes.
MOSCA
Excepting one.
CORVINO   What's that?
MOSCA   Your gallant wife, sir.

                                (*Exit* CORVINO)

Now is he gone; we had no other means
To shoot him hence but this.
VOLPONE   My divine Mosca!
Thou hast today outgone thyself.

                                (*Another knocks*)
                        Who's there?   85

88–9 **The Turk ... Volpone** once again we see that Volpone is not a miser – he is determined to enjoy his wealth.

92 **Or fat, ... man** Volpone is referring to defrauding men of their wealth but the image is one of cannibalism.

98 **Some three hours hence** in keeping with the compactness of the plot, three hours do not elapse until Act 3.

squire her servant.

103–5 **he is politic ... dishonest** in reply to Volpone's wonder at the freedom Englishmen give their wives, Mosca replies that Sir Politic Would-be has no cause for anxiety because, although his spouse is a flirt, she is too ugly for anyone to take her up on her advances. This will give an opportunity for a contrasting description of the beauty of Celia.

108–10 **a wench ... swan** Mosca, in his praise of Celia's beauty, leads Volpone on by suggesting that she is ripe for 'harvest'. He compares her skin to a swan's as a white complexion was much sought after then, so much so that women would moon-bathe in an attempt to get one or use powder to fake the look. Celia, unlike Lady Would-be, needs neither.

I will be troubled with no more. Prepare
Me music, dances, banquets, all delights;
The Turk is not more sensual in his pleasures
Than will Volpone. (*Exit* MOSCA) Let me see, a pearl!
A diamond! plate! chequeens! Good morning's
    purchase;   90
Why, this is better than rob churches yet;
Or fat, by eating once a month a man.
(*Enter* MOSCA)
    Who is't?
MOSCA   The beauteous Lady Would-be, sir.
Wife to the English knight, Sir Politic Would-be,
(This is the style, sir, is directed me)   95
Hath sent to know how you have slept tonight,
And if you would be visited.
VOLPONE   Not now.
Some three hours hence –
MOSCA   I told the squire so much.
VOLPONE
When I am high with mirth and wine, then, then.
'Fore heaven, I wonder at the desperate valour   100
Of the bold English, that they dare let loose
Their wives to all encounters!
MOSCA   Sir, this knight
Had not his name for nothing; he is politic,
And knows, howe'er his wife affect strange airs,
She hath not yet the face to be dishonest.   105
But had she Signior Corvino's wife's face –
VOLPONE
Has she so rare a face?
MOSCA   O, sir, the wonder,
The blazing star of Italy! a wench
O' the first year! a beauty ripe as harvest!
Whose skin is whiter than a swan, all over!   110
Than silver, snow, or lilies! a soft lip,
Would tempt you to eternity of kissing!

114 **Bright as your gold!**   the image is further bait for Volpone and he bites readily.

121 **As the first grapes or cherries**   the image conveys how closely she is guarded, like the first crops of summer.

124–6 **each of which ... examined**   we are given a picture of Corvino's jealousy in that he even pays his servants to spy on each other to ensure no one gets to Celia. Mosca is fully aware of the effect the description will have on a man who loves risk as much as Volpone does.

129 **Maintain mine own shape**   i.e. keep up my guise of being ill. If Volpone is to see Celia, he will have to leave his lair – a disguise will be needed, but the escapade will be fraught with danger as the fox will have been drawn into the open.

And flesh that melteth in the touch to blood!
Bright as your gold! and lovely as your gold!

VOLPONE
Why had not I known this before?

MOSCA   Alas, sir,   115
Myself but yesterday discovered it.

VOLPONE
How might I see her?

MOSCA   O, not possible;
She's kept as warily as is your gold –
Never does come abroad, never takes air
But at a window. All her looks are sweet   120
As the first grapes or cherries – and are watched
As near as they are.

VOLPONE   I must see her –

MOSCA   Sir,
There is a guard, of ten spies thick, upon her –
All his whole household – each of which is set
Upon his fellow, and have all their charge,   125
When he goes out, when he comes in, examined.

VOLPONE
I will go see her, though but at her window.

MOSCA
In some disguise then.

VOLPONE   That is true. I must
Maintain mine own shape still the same; we'll think.

Exeunt

1 *all the world's his soil* all the world is his birthplace (i.e. he is at home anywhere).

3 *if my fates call me forth* if Fortune leads me elsewhere.

4 *no salt desire* no obsession.

5 *shifting a religion* i.e. converting to another religion – an accusation made against travellers was that their contact with other religions often led to conversion (particularly Protestants to Catholicism).

8 *plots* plans.

9–10 *that idle ... with Ulysses* Sir Politic refers to Ulysses' mythological journeying as having an old-fashioned purpose: to explore other cultures. Although this was regarded as the best reason for travel, he is keen to distance himself from anything which might seem out-of-date.

14 *with licence* with permission from the Privy Council (equivalent of a passport).

15 *safelier converse* am less at risk (in your company).

18 *vents our climate* comes from our part of the world (i.e. England).

Act Two

Scene one

The Square, near CORVINO'S *House*
Enter SIR POLITIC WOULD-BE, PEREGRINE
SIR POLITIC
    Sir, to a wise man, all the world's his soil.
    It is not Italy, nor France, nor Europe,
    That must bound me, if my fates call me forth.
    Yet, I protest, it is no salt desire
    Of seeing countries, shifting a religion,   5
    Nor any disaffection to the state
    Where I was bred (and unto which I owe
    My dearest plots) hath brought me out; much less
    That idle, antique, stale, grey-headed project
    Of knowing men's minds and manners, with Ulysses;   10
    But a peculiar humour of my wife's,
    Laid for this height of Venice, to observe,
    To quote, to learn the language, and so forth –
    I hope you travel, sir, with licence?
PEREGRINE   Yes.
SIR POLITIC
    I dare the safelier converse – How long, sir,   15
    Since you left England?
PEREGRINE   Seven weeks.
SIR POLITIC   So lately!
    You ha' not been with my lord ambassador?
PEREGRINE
    Not yet, sir.
SIR POLITIC   Pray you, what news, sir vents our
    climate?
    I heard, last night, a most strange thing reported
    By some of my lord's followers, and I long   20
    To hear how 'twill be seconded.

22–3 **Marry, sir . . . . . King's** Sir Politic is keen to be seen as up-to-date with all the latest news yet shows that he knows nothing more than fantastic gossip. Here he talks of a raven, a bird of ill-omen, building its nest in the king's ship. He sees it as a portend of national disaster.

24 **Does he gull . . . . gulled?** Peregrine is at first unsure as to whether the knight is trying to make a fool of him or is as stupid as he appears. When he learns of the latter's identity, he goes on to amaze him with similar ludicrous stories of wondrous happenings.

25 **O, that speaks him** that says it all.

28 **tires** head-dresses.

29 **courtesans** prostitutes.

30–1 **the spider . . . flower** Peregrine, and the whole of Venice presumably, know of the English lady who, in search of tips on behaviour and dress in the cultural capital of the world, mixes with its prostitutes. Sir Politic defends his wife by referring to an old proverb about the good and bad often feeding from the same source.

34 **your lion's . . . the Tower** according to Stow's Annals, the lioness in the menagerie of the Tower of London whelped in 1604 and 1605. This was a source of much public wonder and some, like Sir Politic, believed it to be a sign.

36–7 **The fires at Berwick . . . star!** in 1604, the appearance of the Northern Lights was mistaken for a ghostly Border battle. In the same year, Kepler, a German astrologer, discovered a new star, which turned out to be a supernova. Again these diverse events were taken as having a meaning by the superstitious.

40–1 **Were there . . . out?** a porpoise was caught in the Thames in 1606. Following this, several sightings of whales and other large mammals caused a public stir. Sir Politic, in his interest and belief in these stories, shows himself to be a superstitious fool.

PEREGRINE   What was't, sir?
SIR POLITIC
   Marry, sir, of a raven, that should build
   In a ship royal of the King's.
PEREGRINE (*Aside*)   –This fellow,
   Does he gull me, trow? or is gulled? – Your name, sir?
SIR POLITIC
   My name is Politic Would-be.
PEREGRINE (*Aside*)   –O, that speaks him –   25
   A knight, sir?
SIR POLITIC   A poor knight, sir.
PEREGRINE   Your lady
   Lies here in Venice, for intelligence
   Of tires, and fashions, and behaviour,
   Among the courtesans? The fine Lady Would-be?
SIR POLITIC
   Yes, sir, the spider and the bee oft-times   30
   Suck from one flower.
PEREGRINE   Good Sir Politic!
   I cry you mercy; I have heard much of you.
   'Tis true, sir, of your raven.
SIR POLITIC   On your knowledge?
PEREGRINE
   Yes, and your lion's whelping in the Tower.
SIR POLITIC
   Another whelp!
PEREGRINE   Another, sir.
SIR POLITIC   Now, heaven!   35
   What prodigies be these? The fires at Berwick!
   And the new star! These things concurring, strange!
   And full of omen! Saw you those meteors?
PEREGRINE
   I did, sir.
SIR POLITIC Fearful! Pray you sir, confirm me,
   Were there three porpoises seen above the bridge,   40
   As they give out?

                                                            77

43 **prodigy** a marvellous thing.

48–9 **for the subversion ... fleet** Peregrine now embellishes the rumours Sir Politic believes by attributing the whale to have been a weapon against the fleet of the English Merchant Adventurers. It was not uncommon at this time for people to believe that animals could be agents of foreign powers – during the Napoleonic wars, a monkey was tried and executed as a spy in the northern town of Hartlepool!

50 **Spain or the Archdukes** King Philip of Spain or his daughter, Isabella, and her husband Albert, rulers of the Spanish Netherlands. Despite the peace treaty of 1604 between England and Spain, many believed the Catholic powers were working to overthrow the Protestant monarchy.

51 **Spinola** commander of the Spanish forces in the Netherlands, believed to be an ingenious military strategist.

53 **Stone the fool** a celebrated fool of this time.

54 **Is Mas' Stone dead?** a hideous pun which Sir Politic is unaware of.

56–9 **O, this knight ... maliciously** the aside is of course Jonson laughing with the audience at his art. Peregrine asserts that if Sir Politic were presented on stage, the author would be derided as creating a caricature: he is deflecting obvious criticism.

62 **He was no kinsman to you?** in the guise of concern, Peregrine is insulting Sir Politic.

PEREGRINE   Six, and a sturgeon, sir.
SIR POLITIC
  I am astonished!
PEREGRINE   Nay, sir, be not so;
  I'll tell you a greater prodigy than these –
SIR POLITIC
  What should these things portend?
PEREGRINE   The very day
  (Let me be sure) that I put forth from London,   45
  There was a whale discovered in the river,
  As high as Woolwich, that had waited there,
  Few know how many months, for the subversion
  Of the Stode fleet.
SIR POLITIC   Is't possible? Believe it,
  'Twas either sent from Spain, or the Archdukes!   50
  Spinola's whale, upon my life, my credit!
  Will they not leave these projects? Worthy sir,
  Some other news.
PEREGRINE   Faith, Stone the fool is dead,
  And they do lack a tavern fool extremely
SIR POLITIC
  Is Mas' Stone dead?
PEREGRINE   He's dead, sir. Why, I hope   55
  You thought him not immortal? (*Aside*) – O, this knight
  (Were he well known) would be a precious thing
  To fit our English stage. He that should write
  But such a fellow, should be thought to feign
  Extremely, if not maliciously.
SIR POLITIC   Stone dead!   60
PEREGRINE
  Dead. Lord! how deeply, sir, you apprehend it!
  He was no kinsman to you?
SIR POLITIC   That I know of.
  Well! that same fellow was an unknown fool.
PEREGINE
  And yet you knew him, it seems?

68–83 **He has received ... cipher**   Sir Politic becomes even more ludicrous, suggesting that the fool was a Dutch (Low Countries) spy, who would receive secret messages hidden in the cabbages imported from that country. He would then pass these on to ambassadors hidden in finer foods. Similarly, he would receive his instructions ('advertisement') in a plate ('trencher') of meat which had been cut up into the shapes of a code ('cipher'), and reply through a toothpick.

85   **In polity**   as a cover.

87   **And to't, as sound a noodle**   and, what's more, had a fine intelligence.

88–9   **your baboons ... China**   Peregrine is tempting the knight with more nonsense.

SIR POLITIC   I did so. Sir,
  I knew him one of the most dangerous heads   65
  Living within the state, and so I held him.
PEREGRINE
  Indeed, sir?
SIR POLITIC   While he lived, in action.
  He has received weekly intelligence,
  Upon my knowledge, out of the Low Countries,
  For all parts of the world, in cabbages;   70
  And those dispensed again to ambassadors,
  In oranges, musk-melons, apricots,
  Lemons, pome-citrons, and such-like – sometimes
  In Colchester oysters, and your Selsey cockles.
PEREGRINE
  You make me wonder!
SIR POLITIC   Sir, upon my knowledge.   75
  Nay, I have observed him, at your public ordinary,
  Take his advertisement, from a traveller
  (A concealed statesman) in a trencher of meat;
  And, instantly, before the meal was done,
  Convey an answer in a toothpick.
PEREGRINE   Strange!   80
  How could this be, sir?
SIR POLITIC   Why, the meat was cut
  So like his character, and so laid, as he
  Must easily read the cipher.
PEREGRINE   I have heard
  He could not read, sir.
SIR POLITIC   So 'twas given out,
  In polity, by those that did employ him;   85
  But he could read, and had your languages,
  And to't, as sound a noddle –
PEREGRINE   I have heard, sir,
  That your baboons were spies; and that they were
  A kind of subtle nation near to China.

90 **Mamuluchi**   slaves who rose to rule Egypt. They have no connection with what has come before but Sir Politic is getting carried away in his desire to impress.

94 *advices*   news.

95 *one of their own coat*   one of their own side.

96 *Made their relations*   made their reports.

101–2 *though I live ... torrent*   the key to his personality – he is an observer, misinterpreting events specifically because he has no part in them. This desire to remain aloof, the fear of being involved, is something which Peregrine will use against him later.

106 *no small tie*   Peregrine, sardonically, thanks his luck for getting him into Sir Politic's company – his motive for doing so is different from what the knight perceives it to be.

113 *that vulgar grammar*   a grammar book.

115 *brave bloods*   young adventurers.

117 *mere bark*   i.e. hollow shells, men of appearance only.

118 *ingenuous race*   noble upbringing.

SIR POLITIC

    Ay, ay, your *Mamuluchi*. Faith, they had   90
    Their hand in a French plot or two; but they
    Were so extremely given to women, as
    They made discovery of all; yet I
    Had my advices here, on Wednesday last,
    From one of their own coat, they were returned,   95
    Made their relations, as the fashion is,
    And now stand fair for fresh employment.

PEREGRINE (*Aside*)   'Heart!
    This Sir Pol will be ignorant of nothing.
    It seems, sir, you know all?

SIR POLITIC   Not all, sir. But
    I have some general notions; I do love   100
    To note and to observe, though I live out,
    Free from the active torrent, yet I'd mark
    The currents and the passages of things,
    For mine own private use; and know the ebbs
    And flows of state.

PEREGRINE   Believe it, sir, I hold   105
    Myself in no small tie unto my fortunes
    For casting me thus luckily upon you;
    Whose knowledge, if your bounty equal it,
    May do me great assistance, in instruction
    For my behaviour, and my bearing, which   110
    Is yet so rude and raw.

SIR POLITIC   Why, came you forth
    Empty of rules for travel?

PEREGRINE   Faith, I had
    Some common ones from out that vulgar grammar
    Which he that cried Italian to me taught me.

SIR POLITIC

    Why, this it is that spoils all our brave bloods;   115
    Trusting our hopeful gentry unto pedants –
    Fellows of outside, and mere bark. You seem
    To be a gentleman, of ingenuous race –

119 **I not profess it**   I do not get paid for it but offer my services voluntarily.

s.d. **mountebank**   this was the name given to the travelling fake doctors, who
would set up a stall in a town square and proceed to con the public into
buying their false cures by using rhetoric, anecdotes and dupes, who
would pretend to be restored to health. The term comes from the fact
that the quacks mounted a bench ('bank') from which to address their
audience.

1 **Under that window**   i.e. Celia's.

3 **dear tongues**   esteemed languages.

5 **quacksalvers**   fake doctors; literally, people who quack about ointments – a
derogatory description.

6 **venting oils**   selling oils.

9 **only knowing men of Europe**   to Sir Politic, the quacks are the most
knowledgeable men in Europe. It is in keeping with his character that he
should be fooled by such fakes and should attempt to 'instruct' the
knowing Peregrine of their worth.

12 **cabinet counsellors**   advisors to the government.

14 **lewd**   ignorant.

15–16 **Made all of ... medicines**   they know only snippets of medical jargon; they lie
as much about the works they have done for great men as they do about
the properties of their medicines.

I not profess it, but my fate hath been
To be where I have been consulted with,   120
In this high kind, touching some great men's sons,
Persons of blood and honour –

PEREGRINE (*Seeing people approach*) Who be these, sir?

Scene two

Enter MOSCA *and* NANO, *disguised as a mountebank's attendants,
with materials for a stage, which they proceed to erect.*

MOSCA
Under that window, there't must be. The same.

SIR POLITIC
Fellows, to mount a bank! Did your instructor
In the dear tongues never discourse to you
Of the Italian mountebanks?

PEREGRINE   Yes, sir.

SIR POLITIC   Why,
Here shall you see one.

PEREGRINE   They are quacksalvers,   5
Fellows that live by venting oils and drugs?

SIR POLITIC
Was that the character he gave you of them?

PEREGRINE
As I remember.

SIR POLITIC   Pity his ignorance.
They are the only knowing men of Europe!
Great general scholars, excellent physicians,   10
Most admired statesmen, professed favourites
And cabinet counsellors to the greatest princes!
The only languaged men of all the world!

PEREGRINE
And I have heard they are most lewd impostors;
Made all of terms, and shreds; no less beliers   15
Of great men's favours than their own vile medicines;

17 *utter*   sell.

19 *crowns*   silver coins worth 25 pence – Peregrine refers to their habit of knocking their prices down to give the appearance of a bargain.

20 *calumnies*   slanders.

22 *Scoto of Mantua*   Volpone has chosen to imitate a famous Italian juggler and magician.

24 *phant'sied*   wrongly described.

26–7 *Here in this nook ... Piazza*   the audience is aware of the reason for the performance being in a remote corner of the city rather than its main square.

28 *zany*   Nano is to be a clown to entertain the audience.

30 *May write ... here*   whose credit is worth 10,000 crowns in the local banks.

31–2 *I do use ... getting up*   I like to watch the ceremony with which he mounts the platform.

36 *the Portico to the Procuratia*   the doorway of the procurator of St Mark's.

Which they will utter, upon monstrous oaths –
Selling that drug for twopence, ere they part,
Which they have valued at twelve crowns before.

SIR POLITIC

Sir, calumnies are answered best with silence.   20
Yourself shall judge. Who is it mounts, my friends?

MOSCA

Scoto of Mantua, sir.

SIR POLITIC   Is't he? Nay, then
I'll proudly promise, sir you shall behold
Another man than has been phant'sied to you.
I wonder, yet, that he should mount his bank   25
Here in this nook, that has been wont t'appear
In face of the Piazza! Here he comes.

Enter VOLPONE, *as a mountebank; a crowd gathers*

VOLPONE (*To* NANO)

Mount, zany.

CROWD   Follow, follow, follow, follow, follow.

SIR POLITIC

See how the people follow him! He's a man
May write ten thousand crowns in bank here. Note,   30
Mark but his gesture! I do use to observe
The state he keeps in getting up!

                                        VOLPONE *mounts the stage*
PEREGRINE   'Tis worth it, sir.

VOLPONE

Most noble gentlemen, and my worthy patrons, it may
seem strange that I, your Scoto Mantuano, who was
ever wont to fix my bank in face of the public Piazza,   35
near the shelter of the Portico to the *Procuratìa*, should
now (after eight months' absence from this illustrious
city of Venice) humbly retire myself into an obscure
nook of the Piazza.

SIR POLITIC

Did not I now object the same?

41 *your Lombard proverb*   an Italian proverb.

42 *cold on my feet*   i.e. without shoes, and so desperate to sell to raise money.

45–6 *Alessandro Buttone*   an imaginary rival.

47 *a* sforzato   as a slave, i.e. by force.

47–8 *Cardinal Bembo*   a renowned humanist of the period. The pause before cook is to suggest that he was about to reveal some sexual association but thought better of it.

50 *ground* ciarlitani   charletans who cannot even afford a bench to work from.

52 *feats of activity*   acrobatic displays.

53 *mouldy*   old; over-told.

Boccaccio   author of the *Decameron*, a collection of a hundred short stories.

53–4 *Tabarine the fabulist*   a contemporary clown.

61 *turdy-facy-nasty ... rogues*   within this outraged description, Volpone turns the nouns 'face' and 'pate' (head) into adjectives in order to sustain the rhythm of the invective.

62–3 *groatsworth ... scartoccios*   antimony is a sulphide which was used in cosmetics and alchemy. Volpone accuses his rivals of being unscrupulous enough to carry one product at a time, using it as a cure-all and disguising it by wrapping it in different covers ('scartoccios').

64 *kill their twenty ... play*   kill twenty people a week yet still prosper.

66 *earthy oppilations*   materialistic thoughts/obstructions.

67 *salad-eating artisans*   i.e. peasants unable to afford meat.

69 *purge 'em into another world*   they seek laxatives but get things which flush them out of this world (i.e. kill them).

PEREGRINE   Peace, sir.   40
VOLPONE

Let me tell you: I am not (as your Lombard proverb
saith) cold on my feet, or content to part with my com-
modities at a cheaper rate than I accustomed – look not
for it. Nor, that the calumnious reports of that impudent
detractor and shame to our profession (Alessandro But-   45
tone, I mean) who gave out, in public, I was con-
demned a *sforzato* to the galleys for poisoning the Cardinal
Bembo's-cook, hath at all attached, much less dejected
me. No, no, worthy gentlemen; to tell you true, I cannot
endure to see the rabble of these ground *ciarlitani*, that   50
spread their cloaks on the pavement as if they meant to
do feats of activity, and then come in lamely with their
mouldy tales out of Boccaccio, like stale Tabarine the
fabulist – some of them discoursing their travels, and of
their tedious captivity in the Turks' galleys, when in-   55
deed (were the truth known) they were the Christians'
galleys, where very temperately they ate bread and
drunk water, as a wholesome penance (enjoined them
by their confessors) for base pilferies.

SIR POLITIC

Note but his bearing, and contempt of these.   60

VOLPONE

These turdy-facy-nasty-paty-lousy-fartical rogues, with
one poor groatsworth of unprepared antimony, finely
wrapped up in several *scartoccios*, are able, very well, to
kill their twenty a week, and play; yet these meagre
starved spirits, who have half stopped the organs of   65
their minds with earthy oppilations, want not their
favourers among your shrivelled, salad-eating artisans,
who are overjoyed that they may have their ha'p'orth of
physic; though it purge 'em into another world, 't makes
no matter.   70

SIR POLITIC

Excellent! Ha' you heard better language, sir?

74 **canaglia**   the common mob.

80–1 *strangers of the Terra Firma*   Venice was detached from the mainland.

84–5 *magazines stuffed with* **moscadelli**   cellars full of Muscatel wines.

87 *cocted*   boiled.

93 *end*   purpose – Peregrine is trying to point out that the mountebank is indulging in salesmanship, making ready for the metaphorical kill but Sir Politic hangs on to the image of him as a straightforward healer.

94 *a humid flux*   a discharge of blood.

94–5 *mutability of air*   change in the climate.

96 *take you ... chequeen*   Volpone picks up his earlier panegyric to health, comparing it to the worthlessness of wealth when illness strikes. His intention is to make his audience see that their own gold would be much better served if exchanged for his oils – he is attempting to dupe them with common sense.

98 **unguento**   oil/ointment.

VOLPONE

Well, let 'em go. And gentlemen, honourable gentlemen, know that for this time our bank, being thus removed from the clamours of the *canaglia*, shall be the
scene of pleasure and delight. For I have nothing to sell,   75
little or nothing to sell.

SIR POLITIC

I told you, sir, his end.

PEREGRINE   You did so, sir.

VOLPONE

I protest, I, and my six servants, are not able to make of
this precious liquor so fast as it is fetched away from my
lodging, by gentlemen of your city, strangers of the Ter-   80
ra Firma, worshipful merchants, ay, and senators too,
who ever since my arrival have detained me to their
uses, by their splendidous liberalities. And worthily.
For what avails your rich man to have his magazines
stuffed with *moscadelli*, or of the purest grape, when his   85
physicians prescribe him – on pain of death – to drink
nothing but water, cocted with aniseeds? O, health!
health! the blessing of the rich! the riches of the poor!
who can buy thee at too dear a rate, since there is no
enjoying this world without thee? Be not then so sparing   90
of your purses, honourable gentlemen, as to abridge the
natural course of life –

PEREGRINE

You see his end?

SIR POLITIC   Ay, is't not good?

VOLPONE

For, when a humid flux, or catarrh, by the mutability of
air, falls from your head into an arm, or shoulder, or   95
any other part, take you a ducat, or your chequeen of
gold, and apply to the place affected: see what good
effect it can work. No, no, 'tis this blessed *unguento*, this
rare extraction, that hath only power to disperse all

100 *malignant humours* a person's temperament was believed to be caused by the balance of the four chief fluids of the body. These were defined as blood, phlegm, choler and melancholy. Diseases arose if this balance was upset.

102 *dry* Peregrine picks up on an error by Volpone in that he used windy not dry as one of the resultant conditions.

106 **vertigine** *in the head* vertigo/dizziness.

108–9 **mal caduco** epilepsy.

110 **tremor-cordia ...** *spleen* heart palpitations, muscle wastage, disorders of the spleen.

111–14 *the strangury ...* **hypocondriaca** difficulty urinating, a hernia leading to flatulence, colic; stops diarrhoea immediately; eases stomach pains; and cures excess of melancholy in the liver, gall-bladder and spleen Volpone does not expect his audience to understand these terms; he is blinding them with science.

119 *Aesculapian art* medical practice.

120 *Zan Fritada* Nano is to play a well-known quack's assistant.

124 *Broughton's books* Broughton was a scholar of the time whose works were regarded as incomprehensible by most people.

malignant humours that proceed either of hot, cold, 100
moist, or windy causes –

PEREGRINE

I would he had put in dry too.

SIR POLITIC   Pray you, observe.

VOLPONE

To fortify the most indigest and crude stomach, ay,
were it of one that through extreme weakness vomited
blood, applying only a warm napkin to the place, after 105
the unction and fricace; for the *vertigine* in the head, putting but a drop into your nostrils, likewise behind the
ears, a most sovereign and approved remedy; the *mal
caduco*, cramps, convulsions, paralyses, epilepsies, *tremor-cordia*, retired nerves, ill vapours of the spleen, stop- 110
pings of the liver, the stone, the strangury, *hernia ventosa,
iliaca passio*; stops a *disenteria* immediately; easeth the
torsion of the small guts; and cures *melancolia hypocondriaca*, being taken and applied, according to my printed
receipt. (*Pointing to his bill and his glass*) For this is the 115
physician, this the medicine; this counsels, this cures;
this gives the direction, this works the effect; and, in
sum, both together may be termed an abstract of the
theoric and practic in the Aesculapian art. 'Twill cost
you eight crowns. And, Zan Fritada, pray thee sing a 120
verse, extempore, in honour of it.

SIR POLITIC

How do you like him, sir?

PEREGRINE   Most strangely, I!

SIR POLITIC

Is not his language rare?

PEREGRINE   But alchemy,

I never heard the like – or Broughton's books.

NANO *sings*

125 *Hippocrates, or Galen*   Greek physicians, the former of whom 'discovered' the humours and their effects.

129 *murderers of so much paper*   i.e. written so much.

130 *hurtless taper*   harmless candle.

132 *sassafras*   like tobacco, recently discovered root which was thought to have medicinal powers.

133 *guacum*   the resin from the guaiacum tree, again believed to have medicinal properties.

134 *Raymond Lully*   the thirteenth-century alchemist who was reputed to have found the elixir of life.

135 *Danish Gonswart*   an imagined figure – his name points to the satirical intent.

136 *Paracelsus*   the pseudonym of Theophrastus Phillipus Aureolus Bombastus von Hohenheim, a sixteenth-century physician who revolutionised the profession by using chemical not herbal remedies. He believed disease came from external causes rather than the humours.

139 **oglio del Scoto**   Scoto's oil.

144–5 *Signiory of the* **Sanità**   the body which oversaw health issues in Venice and granted licences to physicians.

152 *divers*   many.

154 *assayed, like apes*   tried like apes.

Song

Had old Hippocrates, or Galen,   125
(That to their books put med'cines all in)
But known this secret, they had never
(Of which they will be guilty ever)
Been murderers of so much paper,
Or wasted many a hurtless taper;   130
No Indian drug had ere been famèd,
Tobacco, sassafras not namèd;
Ne yet of guacum one small stick, sir,
Nor Raymond Lully's great elixir;
Ne had been known the Danish Gonswart,   135
Or Paracelsus, with his long sword.

PEREGRINE

All this, yet, will not do; eight crowns is high.

VOLPONE

No more. Gentlemen, if I had but time to discourse to
you the miraculous effects of this my oil, surnamed *oglio
del Scoto*; with the countless catalogue of those I have   140
cured of th'aforesaid and many more diseases; the pa-
tents and privileges of all the princes and common-
wealths of Christendom; or but the depositions of those
that appeared on my part before the Signiory of the
Sanità and most learned college of physicians; where I   145
was authorized, upon notice taken of the admirable virtues of my medicaments, and mine own excellency in
matter of rare and unknown secrets, not only to disperse
them publicly in this famous city, but in all the territor-
ies that happily joy under the government of the most   150
pious and magnificent states of Italy. But may some
other gallant fellow say, 'O, there be divers that make
profession to have as good and as experimented receipts
as yours.' Indeed, very many have assayed, like apes, in
imitation of that which is really and essentially in me, to   155

157 **alembics** distilling vessels.

158–9 **several simples** different herbal ingredients.

160 **conglutination** sticking together.

161 **decoction** boiling to extract the essence of a drug or medicinal plant.

162 **in fumo** in a puff of smoke

167 **book them** record them.

175 **balloo** a ball game played in Venice.

179 **And that withal** once again, Peregrine draws Sir Politic's attention to the mountebank's intent.

181 **ampulla** container

187 **the Cardinals Montalto, Fernese** historical figures, the former of whom became Pope.

make of this oil; bestowed great cost in furnaces, stills,
alembics, continual fires and preparation of the ingredients (as indeed there goes to it six hundred several
simples, besides some quantity of human fat, for the
conglutination, which we buy of the anatomists), but,   160
when these practitioners come to the last decoction,
blow, blow, puff, puff, and all flies in *fumo*. Ha, ha, ha!
Poor wretches! I rather pity their folly and indiscretion
than their loss of time and money; for those may be recovered by industry, but to be a fool born is a disease   165
incurable. For my self, I always from my youth have
endeavoured to get the rarest secrets, and book them;
either in exchange, or for money; I spared nor cost nor
labour where anything was worthy to be learned. And
gentlemen, honourable gentlemen, I will undertake, by   170
virtue of chemical art, out of the honourable hat that
covers your head, to extract the four elements – that is
to say, the fire, air, water, and earth – and return you
your felt without burn or stain. For, whilst others have
been at the *balloo*, I have been at my book; and am now   175
past the craggy paths of study, and come to the flowery
plains of honour and reputation.

SIR POLITIC

I do assure you, sir, that is his aim.

VOLPONE

But, to our price –

PEREGRINE   And that withal, Sir Pol.

VOLPONE

You all know, honourable gentlemen, I never valued   180
this *ampulla*, or vial, at less than eight crowns; but for
this time I am content to be deprived of it for six; six
crowns is the price; and less, in courtesy, I know you
cannot offer me; take it or leave it, howsoever, both it,
and I, am at your service. I ask you not as the value of   185
the thing, for then I should demand of you a thousand
crowns, so the Cardinals Montalto, Fernese, the great

188 *my gossip*   my intimate relation/godfather.

197 *painful circumstance*   painstaking performance (for so little reward).

204 *Tart of palate*   a good sense of taste.

205 *Moist of hand*   associated with sexual prowess.

208 *Do the act your mistress pleases*   again the oil is said to increase sexual performance.

210 *for the nones*   for this purpose.

217 *nor half a ducat ... moccenigo*   these are relatively small sums, the last in a steadily decreasing scale as the mountebank knocks his price down to entice his audience.

Duke of Tuscany, my gossip, with divers other princes
have given me; but I despise money. Only to show my
affection to you, honourable gentlemen, and your illus-   190
trious state here, I have neglected the messages of these
princes, mine own offices, framed my journey hither,
only to present you with the fruits of my travels. (*To*
NANO *and* MOSCA) Tune your voices once more to the
touch of your instruments, and give the honourable   195
assembly some delightful recreation.

PEREGRINE

What monstrous and most painful circumstance
Is here, to get some three or four *gazets*!
Some threepence i'th' whole, for that 'twill come to.

Song

> You that would last long, list to my song: 200
> Make no more coil, but buy of this oil.
> Would you be ever fair? and young?
> Stout of teeth? and strong of tongue?
> Tart of palate? quick of ear?
> Moist of hand? and light of foot?   205
> Or, I will come nearer to't –
> Would you live free from all diseases?
> Do the act your mistress pleases;
> Yet fright all achès from your bones?
> Here's a med'cine for the nones.   210

VOLPONE

Well, I am in a humour, at this time, to make a present
of the small quantity my coffer contains: to the rich, in
courtesy, and to the poor, for God's sake. Wherefore,
now mark; I asked you six crowns; and six crowns at
other times you have paid me; you shall not give me six   215
crowns, nor five, nor four, nor three, nor two, nor one;
nor half a ducat; no, nor a *moccenigo*; six – pence it will

219 **the banner of my front**   his advertising banner.

    bate a bagatine   reduce the price by the smallest amount.

227 **a double pistolet**   a valuable gold coin.

230 **I kiss your bounty**   I kiss your kind gift.

236–7 **if I should ... worth**   if I should describe its worth.

247 **derived to Helen**   passed to Helen of Troy – just like the soul of Pythagoras, the powder descends the social scale as it comes to modern times. (See also note to Act 1, scene 2, lines 8–21.)

249 **a studious antiquary**   a studious archaeologist.

250 **moiety**   part.

cost you, or six hundred pound – expect no lower price,
for by the banner of my front, I will not bate a *bagatine*;
that I will have, only, a pledge of your loves, to carry   220
something from amongst you, to show I am not con-
temned by you. Therefore now, toss your handkerchiefs,
cheerfully, cheerfully; and be advertised, that the first
heroic spirit that deigns to grace me with a handkerchief, I will give it a little remembrance of something   225
beside, shall please it better than if I had presented it
with a double pistolet.

PEREGRINE

Will you be that heroic spark, Sir Pol?
O, see! the window has prevented you.

           CELIA *at the window throws down her handkerchief*

VOLPONE

Lady, I kiss your bounty; and for this timely grace you   230
have done your poor Scoto of Mantua, I will return you,
over and above my oil, a secret of that high and inestim-
able nature shall make you for ever enamoured on that
minute wherein your eye first descended on so mean
(yet not altogether to be despised) an object. Here is a   235
powder, concealed in this paper, of which, if I should
speak to the worth, nine thousand volumes were but as
one page, that page as a line, that line as a word – so
short is this pilgrimage of man (which some call life) to
the expressing of it. Would I reflect on the price, why!   240
the whole world were but as an empire, that empire as a
province, that province as a bank, that bank as a private
purse, to the purchase of it. I will only tell you: it is the
powder that made Venus a goddess (given her by Apollo), that kept her perpetually young, cleared her wrink-   245
les, firmed her gums, filled her skin, coloured her hair;
from her, derived to Helen, and at the sack of Troy un-
fortunately lost; till now, in this our age, it was as happily recovered by a studious antiquary out of some ruins
of Asia, who sent a moiety of it to the court of France   250

101

251 **sophisticated**   adulterated.

253 **extracted to a quintessence**   refined to its purest form.

256 **like virginal jacks**   this refers to the virginal, a small harpsichord, whose keys
were called jacks.

3–8 **Signior Flaminio ... sir?**   Corvino, in his rage, portrays the scene as one from
the *commedia dell'arte*, popular Italian comedy in which players acted out
farces for the public enjoyment. He sees those present as the stock
characters used: the mountebank is Signior Flaminio, the lover; Celia is
Franciscina, the unfaithful maid and he is Pantalone di Besogniosi, the 'lean
and slippered merchant cuckolded by his younger wife'. The public
disgrace he imagines is nothing compared to that he will soon bring upon
himself.

10 **Some trick of state**   it is typical of Sir Politic that he will see this domestic
dispute as having political meaning, as possibly a plot against himself.
Peregrine encourages him to think for his own pleasure.

(but much sophisticated), wherewith the ladies there
now colour their hair. The rest, at this present, remains
with me, extracted to a quintessence, so that, wherever
it but touches, in youth it perpetually preserves, in age
restores the complexion; seats your teeth, did they   255
dance like virginal jacks, firm as a wall; makes them
white as ivory, that were black as –

Scene three

Enter CORVINO

CORVINO

   Blood o' the devil, and my shame! come down here;
   Come down! No house but mine to make your scene?
                (*He beats away the mountebank, & c.*)
   Signior Flaminio, will you down, sir? down?
   What, is my wife your Franciscina, sir?
   No windows on the whole piazza here   5
   To make your properties, but mine? but mine?
   Heart! ere tomorrow I shall be new christened,
   And called the *Pantalone di Besogniosi*
   About the town.

                                                Exit

PEREGRINE   What should this mean, Sir Pol?

SIR POLITIC

   Some trick of state, believe it. I will home.   10

PEREGRINE

   It may be some design on you.

SIR POLITIC   I know not.

   I'll stand upon my guard.

PEREGRINE   It is your best, sir.

SIR POLITIC

   This three weeks, all my advices, all my letters,
   They have been intercepted.

PEREGRINE   Indeed, sir?

3 **bolting**   shooting an arrow. Volpone has been shot by the god of love.

5–7 **his burning heat ... stopped**   Volpone compares the love he now feels to a
fire which gains in intensity because it is confined in a small space. The
image does not quite work, because fires need air and fuel, but it conveys
his meaning, he is suffering because he cannot vent his passion on Celia.

9 **My liver melts**   the liver, the source of passion, is melting with the heat.

Best have a care.

SIR POLITIC   Nay, so I will.

Exit   *Exit*

PEREGRINE   This knight,   15
  I may not lose him, for my mirth, till night.

                                                                Exit

Scene four

Enter VOLPONE, MOSCA

VOLPONE

  O, I am wounded.

MOSCA   Where, sir?

VOLPONE   Not without;
  Those blows were nothing – I could bear them ever.
  But angry Cupid, bolting from her eyes,
  Hath shot himself into me like a flame,
  Where now he flings about his burning heat,   5
  As in a furnace an ambitious fire
  Whose vent is stopped. The fight is all within me.
  I cannot live, except thou help me, Mosca;
  My liver melts, and I, without the hope
  Of some soft air from her refreshing breath,   10
  Am but a heap of cinders.

MOSCA   'Las, good sir!
  Would you had never seen her.

VOLPONE   Nay, would thou
  Hadst never told me of her.

MOSCA   Sir, 'tis true;
  I do confess, I was unfortunate,
  And you unhappy: but I'm bound in conscience,   15
  No less than duty, to effect my best
  To your release of torment, and I will, sir.

20 **Within a human compass** within the human sphere – Mosca is confident of his ability to achieve anything.

21 **My better angel** in many respects, Volpone is aware of the irony of this complement as Mosca is more like his master's bad angel. He intends to use him to sin further.

22 **devotion** disposal. Volpone deliberately uses the word because of its religious connotations. Restored to sense after his initial despair, he is able to mock contemporary morality once more.

23–4 **coin me ... longings** the pun here centres around Volpone giving Mosca permission to convert him into money in order to fulfil ('crown') his desires. He is simply playing on words.

28 **horn him** to make him a cuckold It was a literary tradition that victims of adultery were said to wear horns on their head.

34 **Escape your epilogue** Mosca is careful not to enrage Volpone by suggesting that he too would like to bed Celia.

37 **I have not ... now** having just flattered Volpone, Mosca denies that he has the time to do this. His skill lies in exploiting his master's weakness for praise but disguising when he is flattering him. In this way he can appear to be a sincere admirer of his master as well as a paid lackey.

VOLPONE

Dear Mosca, shall I hope?

MOSCA   Sir, more than dear,

I will not bid you to despair of aught,

Within a human compass.

VOLPONE   O, there spoke   20

My better angel. Mosca, take my keys,

Gold, plate, and jewels, all's at thy devotion;

Employ them how thou wilt; nay, coin me, too,

So thou, in this, but crown my longings. – Mosca?

MOSCA

Use but your patience.

VOLPONE   So I have.

MOSCA   I doubt not   25

To bring success to your desires.

VOLPONE   Nay, then,

I not repent me of my late disguise.

MOSCA

If you can horn him, sir, you need not.

VOLPONE   True.

Besides, I never meant him for my heir.

Is not the colour o' my beard and eyebrows   30

To make me known?

MOSCA   No jot.

VOLPONE   I did it well.

MOSCA

So well, would I could follow you in mine

With half the happiness; and yet, I would

Escape your epilogue.

VOLPONE   But were they gulled

With a belief that I was Scoto?

MOSCA   Sir,   35

Scoto himself could hardly have distinguished!

I have not time to flatter you now. We'll part;

And, as I prosper, so applaud my art.

Exeunt

2   ***A juggling ... mountebank?***   Corvino is still railing against the mountebank.

   tooth-drawing   mountebanks frequently acted as dentists too.

4   ***dole***   repertoire.

5   ***itching***   eager.

7   ***satyrs***   mythological creatures, half-man, half-beast, known for their lasciviousness.

8   ***fan your favours forth***   Corvino wrongly accuses his wife of enticing the crowd with favourable glances.

9   ***hot***   with lust.

11–14   ***enamoured ... feather***   his jealously is revealed by his description of the mountebank, which pictures him as showy, dressed in cheap jewellery and clothes.

12   ***saffron jewel***   an orange-coloured trinket – fake gold.

   toad-stone   the stone found between a toad's eyes was thought to be magical.

13–14   ***cope-stitch ... hearse-cloth***   he accuses the mountebank of using a fancy stitch to hide the fact that his garments are made from funeral pall.

14   ***tilt-feather***   fools were thought to wear feathers in their caps.

17   ***The fricace, ... mother***   ostensibly, a massage for hysteria but Corvino is being crude as this ailment was believed to begin in the womb. As elsewhere in this diatribe, he shows himself to be obsessed with the idea of Celia having sexual intercourse with another man.

18   ***mount***   literally, mount the bench but intended to have a sexual meaning.

20   ***down to th' foot***   if she were up on a bench, she could be seen completely from head to foot; just so, if she was having sexual intercourse.

21   ***cittern***   guitar-like instrument played by mountebank's assistants and prostitutes.

23–4   ***Make one ... a Dutchman, I!***   join him! I'll announce that I am a cuckold and you will have forfeited your dowry. He goes on to say that she must think he has the patience of a Dutchman rather than the temper of an Italian. Ironically Corvone is describing the disgrace he will later bring upon himself.

Scene five

CORVINO'S *House*
Enter CORVINO, CELIA

CORVINO

    Death of mine honour, with the city's fool?
    A juggling, tooth-drawing, prating mountebank?
    And at a public window? where, whilst he,
    With his strained action and his dole of faces,
    To his drug lecture draws your itching ears,   5
    A crew of old, unmarried, noted lechers
    Stood leering up, like satyrs; and you smile,
    Most graciously! and fan your favours forth,
    To give your hot spectators satisfaction!
    What, was your mountebank their call? their whistle?   10
    Or were you enamoured on his copper rings?
    His saffron jewel, with the toad-stone in't?
    Or his embroidered suit, with the cope-stitch,
    Made of a hearse-cloth? or his old tilt-feather?
    Or his starched beard? Well! you shall have him, yes.   15
    He shall come home, and minister unto you
    The fricace, for the mother. Or, let me see,
    I think you'd rather mount? Would you not mount?
    Why, if you'll mount, you may; yes truly, you may;
    And so you may be seen, down to th'foot.   20
    Get you a cittern, Lady Vanity,
    And be a dealer with the virtuous man;
    Make one – I'll but protest myself a cuckold,
    And save your dowry. I am a Dutchman, I!
    For, if you thought me an Italian,   25
    You would be damned ere you did this, you whore!
    Thou'dst tremble to imagine that the murder
    Of father, mother, brother, all thy race,
    Should follow as the subject of my justice.

CELIA

    Good sir, have patience!

34 **goatish** goats were associated with lust.

38 **a parley** a conversation.

44 **might serve the turn** i.e. offer a place to have sex.

47 **Well, it shall be less** we already know how closely he keeps Celia guarded. This new threat serves only to highlight the cruelty and stupidity of the man.

50 **this bawdy light** i.e. the window. He accuses her of using it like a whore's signal.

55–6 **conjurer ... was laid** a magician could summon demons and as long as he remained within his circle he was safe until he sent them back to hell.

57 **a lock** a chastity belt, designed to prevent sexual intercourse.

58 **backwards** at the back of the house.

CORVINO   What couldst thou propose   30
    Less to thyself, than, in this heat of wrath,
    And stung with my dishonour, I should strike
                (*Threatening her with his sword*)
    This steel into thee, with as many stabs
    As thou wert gazed upon with goatish eyes?

CELIA
    Alas, sir, be appeased! I could not think   35
    My being at the window should more now
    Move your impatience than at other times.

CORVINO
    No? not to seek and entertain a parley
    With a known knave? before a multitude?
    You were an actor, with your handkerchief!   40
    Which he, most sweetly, kissed in the receipt,
    And might, no doubt, return it with a letter,
    And point the place where you might meet; your
      sister's,
    Your mother's, or your aunt's might serve the turn.

CELIA
    Why, dear sir, when do I make these excuses?   45
    Or ever stir abroad but to the church?
    And that so seldom –

CORVINO   Well, it shall be less;
    And thy restraint before was liberty
    To what I now decree, and therefore, mark me:
    First, I will have this bawdy light dammed up;   50
    And, till't be done, some two or three yards off,
    I'll chalk a line; o'er which if thou but chance
    To set thy desp'rate foot, more hell, more horror,
    More wild remorseless rage shall seize on thee
    Than on a conjurer that had heedless left   55
    His circle's safety ere his devil was laid.
    Then, here's a lock, which I will hang upon thee;
    And, now I think on't, I will keep thee backwards;
    Thy lodging shall be backwards; thy walks backwards;

64–6 **your subtle ... passengers** the image is a repulsive one of Celia sniffing out passers-by as if on heat.

70 **I will make thee an anatomy** I will dissect you.

1–2 **His master's ... bad** his master's dead. At last some good news to go with the bad.

Thy prospect – all be backwards; and no pleasure   60
That thou shalt know, but backwards. Nay, since you
    force
My honest nature, know it is your own
Being too open, makes me use you thus.
Since you will not contain your subtle nostrils
In a sweet room, but they must snuff the air   65
Of rank and sweaty passengers –

                                    (*Knock within*)
                        One knocks.
Away, and be not seen, pain of thy life;
Not look toward the window; if thou dost –
Nay, stay, hear this – let me not prosper, whore,
But I will make thee an anatomy,   70
Dissect thee mine own self, and read a lecture
Upon thee to the city, and in public.
Away! (*Exit* CELIA) Who's there?
Enter SERVANT

SERVANT   'Tis Signior Mosca, sir.

Scene six

CORVINO

Let him come in. (*Exit* SERVANT)
                        His master's dead. There's yet
Some good, to help the bad. (*Enter* MOSCA)
                                My Mosca, welcome –
I guess your news.

MOSCA   I fear you cannot, sir.

CORVINO

Is't not his death?

MOSCA   Rather the contrary.

CORVINO

Not his recovery?

MOSCA   Yes, sir.

113

6 **my crosses meet to vex me** i.e. all my afflictions come at once. The word has religious connotations and is used in a blasphemous way. The irony is that the elements Corvino complains of here will prove to be his own doing; they will be the agents of retribution.

7 **Scoto's oil** Mosca cannot resist this last touch – to make the mountbanke's fake cure the supposed restorative of Volpone. It is designed to drive Corvino to distraction.

14 **th'osteria** an inn.

15 **forced** pathetically contrived.

16 **dead wine** i.e. dregs.

19 **sod** boiled.

20 **fasting spittle** the spittle of someone who is fasting, i.e. his own.

24 **fricace** see note to scene 5, line 17. Mosca inadvertently employs the word Corvino has previously used as a euphemism for sexual intercourse. It enrages the latter more.

25 **officious** dutiful.

29 **a cataplasm** a poultice.

29–35 **Where one ... by him** once again the medical profession is held up to ridicule. The suggestion implicit is that doctors are as much quacks as Scoto.

35 **Lusty, and full of juice** i.e. young and fertile. The suggestion that the two qualities will rub off in some way is so ludicrous that Corvino will not fall for it – which is precisely what Mosca wants. By convincing him that Volpone will die, rather than be healed by the experience, he will get his approval for Celia to be the girl.

CORVINO   I am cursed,   5
  I am bewitched, my crosses meet to vex me.
  How? how? how? how?
MOSCA   Why, sir, with Scoto's oil!
  Corbaccio and Voltore brought of it,
  Whilst I was busy in an inner room –
CORVINO
  Death! that damned mountebank! But for the law,   10
  Now I could kill the rascal; 't cannot be
  His oil should have that virtue. Ha' not I
  Known him a common rogue, come fiddling in
  To th'*osteria* with a tumbling whore,
  And, when he has done all his forced tricks, been glad   15
  Of a poor spoonful of dead wine, with flies in't?
  It cannot be. All his ingredients
  Are a sheep's gall, a roasted bitch's marrow,
  Some few sod earwigs, pounded caterpillars,
  A little capon's grease, and fasting spittle –   20
  I know 'em to a dram.
MOSCA   I know not, sir,
  But some on't, there, they poured into his ears,
  Some in his nostrils, and recovered him,
  Applying but the fricace.
CORVINO   Pox o' that fricace.
MOSCA
  And since, to seem the more officious   25
  And flattering of his health, there they have had,
  At extreme fees, the college of physicians
  Consulting on him, how they might restore him;
  Where one would have a cataplasm of spices,
  Another, a flayed ape clapped to his breast,   30
  A third would ha' it a dog, a fourth an oil
  With wild cats' skins; at last, they all resolved
  That to preserve him was no other means
  But some young woman must be straight sought out,
  Lusty, and full of juice, to sleep by him;   35

115

40–1 **might cross Your ends**   might destroy your purposes i.e. to be Volpone's heir.

42 **delate**   report.

47 **present him**   i.e. with a bed companion.

51 **courtesan**   prostitute.

51–5 **Ay, I thought . . . us all**   Mosca's planning is so thorough that he has foreseen this suggestion and now negates it by saying that a cunning prostitute might easily sway the fickle old man to change his will in her favour.

57 **a creature made unto it**   someone suited to the task.

59 **Think, think, think . . .**   Mosca has suggested a kinsman and now harries Corvino to come up with the answer he wants by pretending to be desperately searching for the answer. The repetition heightens the sense of urgency.

61 **Lupo**   a surname meaning wolf.

62 **And a virgin, sir**   this adds a new twist, which is that Volpone is too feeble to have sex with the girl chosen. A man would not allow his daughter to lose her virginity as this would destroy her value in the marriage market.

And to this service – most unhappily
And most unwillingly – am I now employed,
Which here I thought to pre-acquaint you with,
For your advice, since it concerns you most,
Because I would not do that thing might cross   40
Your ends, on whom I have my whole dependence, sir.
Yet, if I do it not, they may delate
My slackness to my patron, work me out
Of his opinion; and there, all your hopes,
Ventures, or whatsoever, are all frustrate.   45
I do but tell you, sir. Besides, they are all
Now striving, who shall first present him. Therefore –
I could entreat you, briefly, conclude somewhat;
Prevent 'em if you can.
CORVINO   Death to my hopes!
This is my villainous fortune! Best to hire   50
Some common courtesan?
MOSCA   Ay, I thought on that, sir.
But they are all so subtle, full of art,
And age again doting and flexible,
So as – I cannot tell – we may perchance
Light on a quean, may cheat us all.
CORVINO   'Tis true.   55
MOSCA
No, no; it must be one that has no tricks, sir,
Some simple thing, a creature made unto it;
Some wench you may command. Ha' you no
    kinswoman?
God's so – Think, think, think, think, think, think,
    think, sir.
One o' the doctors offered there his daughter.   60
CORVINO
How?
MOSCA   Yes, Signior Lupo, the physician.
CORVINO
His daughter!
MOSCA   And a virgin, sir. Why! Alas,

64 **That naught ... fever**   this picks up the earlier image of passion being like a fire. Mosca pictures Volpone as being impotent.

66 **that part**   i.e. his penis.

68–9 **If any man ... luck**   if anyone else was in my position. Corvino is talking himself around to offering Celia.

74 **I hear him coming**   i.e. round to the idea.

75 **who is not engaged**   i.e. has not yet staked anything on Volpone's death.

79 **Covetous wretch!**   Corvino is so steeped in greed that he is blind to his own failings. The accusation against the fictional Lupo is heavily ironic.

80 **wot of**   have talked of.

83 **motioned**   suggested. Mosca has, of course, guided him to precisely this decision.

84 **make your count**   count your riches, i.e. you have guaranteed yourself his heir.

86 **we may let him go**   allow him to die – a euphemism for murder!

90 **My conscience fools my wit**   this from a man who has virtually agreed to prostitute his wife!

He knows the state of 's body, what it is;
That naught can warm his blood, sir, but a fever;
Nor any incantation raise his spirit –   65
A long forgetfulness hath seized that part.
Besides, sir, who shall know it? some one, or two –

CORVINO

I pray thee give me leave. (*Walks aside*) If any man
But I had had this luck – The thing in't self,
I know, is nothing – Wherefore should not I   70
As well command my blood and my affections
As this dull doctor? In the point of honour,
The cases are all one of wife and daughter.

MOSCA

(*Aside*) I hear him coming.

CORVINO   She shall do't; 'tis done.
'Slight, if this doctor, who is not engaged,   75
Unless't be for his counsel (which is nothing),
Offer his daughter, what should I, that am
So deeply in? I will prevent him – wretch!
Covetous wretch! Mosca, I have determined.

MOSCA

How, sir?

CORVINO   We'll make all sure. The party you
    wot of   80
Shall be mine own wife, Mosca.

MOSCA   Sir, the thing
(But that I would not seem to counsel you)
I should have motioned to you at the first;
And, make your count, you have cut all their throats.
Why, 'tis directly taking a possession!   85
And, in his next fit, we may let him go.
'Tis but to pull the pillow from his head,
And he is throttled – 't had been done before,
But for your scrupulous doubts.

CORVINO   Ay, a plague on't,
My conscience fools my wit. Well, I'll be brief,   90

119

95 **free motion** like Corbaccio in the matter of the will, Corvino is sure he has come up with the scheme himself; such is Mosca's skill as a manipulator. It is fitting that both men claim credit for the intrigues which will destroy their reputations and lead to public disgrace.

96 **posses** make him aware of.

100 **ripen** hatch. Mosca is simply making time to put his other plot into action.

5 **confirmed thee** assured you. Corvino must now change his tune to get Celia to agree to that which he accused her of earlier. It is a mark of the man's irrationality that, having branded her a whore, he foresees that she will be unwilling to go to bed with Volpone and so hides this from her; it is a mark of his hypocrisy that he still talks of woman's lack of constancy whilst planning to give her to another man.

7 **unprofitable humour** his mind set on gold, he means this literally. Corvino obviously has no true sense of morality and worried about being a cuckold simply because of the damage it would do to his reputation.

And so be thou, lest they should be before us;
Go home, prepare him, tell him with what zeal
And willingness I do it; swear it was
On the first hearing – as thou mayst do, truly –
Mine own free motion.

MOSCA   Sir, I warrant you,   95
I'll so possess him with it that the rest
Of his starved clients shall be banished, all,
And only you received. But come not, sir,
Until I send, for I have something else
To ripen for your good – you must not know't.   100

CORVINO

But do not you forget to send, now.

MOSCA   Fear not.

                              (*Exit* MOSCA)

Scene seven

CORVINO

Where are you, wife? my Celia? wife?
(*Enter* CELIA *weeping*)

                              What, blubbering?
Come, dry those tears. I think thou thought'st me in
    earnest?
Ha? By this light, I talked so but to try thee.
Methinks the lightness of the occasion
Should ha' confirmed thee. Come I am not jealous.   5

CELIA

No?

CORVINO Faith, I am not, I, nor never was;
It is a poor, unprofitable humour.
Do not I know, if women have a will,
They'll do 'gainst all the watches o' the world?
And that the fiercest spies are tamed with gold?   10
Tut, I am confident in thee, thou shalt see't;

17–18 ***where it . . . or fear*** given his intent, the light tone of this assurance is sickening to the audience.

And see, I'll give thee cause too, to believe it.
Come, kiss me. Go, and make thee ready straight
In all thy best attire thy choicest jewels,
Put 'em all on, and with 'em, thy best looks;   15
We are invited to a solemn feast
At old Volpone's, where it shall appear
How far I am free from jealousy or fear.

Exeunt

2 *prosp'rous parts* profitable abilities. Mosca will go on to claim that his servility is nothing more than an act, something he can switch on and off at will.

3 *burgeon* flourish.

4 *A whimsy i' my blood* a feeling of elation flowing through me.

5 *wanton* playful.

6 *subtle snake* a fitting animal image, capturing both his cunning and his lack of loyalty to anything but himself.

8 *dropped from above* i.e. a gift from heaven. The irony of this remark is evident to the audience, if not to the speaker.

9 *clotpoles* idiots.

11 *liberally professed* widely practised.

13 *sub-parasites* Mosca will draw a distinction between those born to be parasites and poor imitators in an attempt to give himself greater status.

14 *your bare town-art* limited skills of those who must grovel to feed themselves.

17 *to bait that sense* tempt them; trap them.

18 *Kitchen-invention ... receipts* servants' food or stale scraps.

20 *court-dog-tricks* Mosca compares courtiers to performing dogs. Scorn of these was common at this time and they are frequently ridiculed in plays e.g. Osric in Hamlet.

20 *fleer* smile.

21-2 *Make their revènue ... moth* make their money by bows and smiling, agreeing with everything their master says and constantly flattering. The final image picks up the contemporary slang of 'licking' meaning crawling: the courtiers are so constantly obsequious that even an insect cannot get close to their master.

23-7 *But your fine ... at once* the images Mosca uses for himself are important because all convey his independence: not for him the master's chain, he values too much his ability to soar. At face value, this means that one of the reasons he serves Volpone is that he likes the opportunity to exercise his own intelligence which his master's love of risk presents.

Act Three

Scene one

A Street
Enter MOSCA
MOSCA
    I fear I shall begin to grow in love
    With my dear self and my most prosp'rous parts,
    They do so spring and burgeon; I can feel
    A whimsy i' my blood. I know not how,
    Success hath made me wanton. I could skip   5
    Out of my skin, now, like a subtle snake,
    I am so limber. O! your parasite
    Is a most precious thing, dropped from above,
    Not bred 'mongst clods and clotpoles, here on earth.
    I muse the mystery was not made a science,   10
    It is so liberally professed! Almost
    All the wise world is little else in nature
    But parasites, or sub-parasites. And yet,
    I mean not those that have your bare town-art,
    To know who's fit to feed 'em; have no house,   15
    No family, no care, and therefore mould
    Tales for men's ears, to bait that sense; or get
    Kitchen-invention, and some stale receipts
    To please the belly, and the groin; nor those,
    With their court-dog-tricks, that can fawn and fleer,   20
    Make their revènue out of legs and faces,
    Echo my lord, and lick away a moth;
    But your fine, elegant rascal, that can rise
    And stoop (almost together) like an arrow;
    Shoot through the air as nimbly as a star;   25
    Turn short, as doth a swallow; and be here,
    And there, and here, and yonder, all at once;
    Present to any humour, all occasion;

29 **visor**   mask.

32 ***Out of most excellent nature***   as a gift from nature; with excellent natural
   ability.

   sparks   young gallants, men-about-town.

33 **zanie**   clowns; buffoons.

? **bound**   on my way.

11 ***Thy means of feeding?***   the question links Mosca to the animalistic parasite
   and gives a stunning contrast to the panegyric he has just given on himself.
   This is how true 'sparks' see his role.

12–13 ***These imputations ... she's poor***   these false accusations are too widely
   believed and stick to us simply because we are poor. Mosca is play-acting
   the virtuous man in order to trap Bonario.

15–16 ***yet you ... censure***   Mosca chides Bonario for condemning him before he
   truly knows him. He pretends to be wounded by the accusations.

And change a visor swifter than a thought!
This is the creature, had the art born with him; 30
Toils not to learn it, but doth practise it
Out of most excellent nature; and such sparks
Are the true parasites, others but their zanies.

Scene two

Enter BONARIO

MOSCA
  Who's this? Bonario? old Corbaccio's son?
  The person I was bound to seek. Fair sir,
  You are happ'ly met.
BONARIO   That cannot be by thee.
MOSCA
  Why, sir?
BONARIO   Nay, pray thee know thy way, and leave me;
  I would be loath to interchange discourse 5
  With such a mate as thou art.
MOSCA   Courteous sir,
  Scorn not my poverty.
BONARIO   Not I, by heaven –
  But thou shalt give me leave to hate thy baseness.
MOSCA
  Baseness?
BONARIO   Ay, answer me, is not thy sloth
  Sufficient argument? thy flattery? 10
  Thy means of feeding?
MOSCA   Heaven, be good to me!
  These imputations are too common, sir,
  And eas'ly stuck on virtue when she's poor;
  You are unequal to me, and howe'er
  Your sentence may be righteous, yet you are not, 15
  That ere you know me, thus proceed in censure.
  St Mark bear witness 'gainst you, 'tis inhuman.

Weeps

22 **obsequy**   deference.

23 **spin mine own poor raiment**   make my own living.

25–34 **But that I ... goodness**   it is hard not to be impressed by his audacity as here, in a feigned fit of moral anger, he denies doing the very things he takes most pride in. His scorn of the easy life and praise of hard work are laughable, and intended to be so – Mosca is enjoying himself.

35 **personated passion!**   simulated anguish – Bonario's virtue and naivety make him easy prey for Mosca. Venice is a land where to be noble is to be weak, such is the corruption which abounds.

46 **engageth**   concerns; involves.

BONARIO (*Aside*)
What? does he weep? the sign is soft and good!
I do repent me that I was so harsh.

MOSCA
'Tis true that, swayed by strong necessity,   20
I am enforced to eat my careful bread
With too much obsequy; 'tis true, beside,
That I am fain to spin mine own poor raiment
Out of my mere observance, being not born
To a free fortune. But that I have done   25
Base offices, in rending friends asunder,
Dividing families, betraying counsels,
Whispering false lies, or mining men with praises,
Trained their credulity with perjuries,
Corrupted chastity, or am in love   30
With mine own tender ease, but would not rather
Prove the most rugged and laborious course
That might redeem my present estimation,
Let me here perish, in all hope of goodness.

BONARIO (*Aside*)
This cannot be a personated passion! –   35
I was to blame, so to mistake thy nature;
Pray thee forgive me, and speak out thy business.

MOSCA
Sir, it concerns you; and though I may seem
At first, to make a main offence in manners,
And in my gratitude unto my master,   40
Yet, for the pure love which I bear all right,
And hatred of the wrong, I must reveal it.
This very hour, your father is in purpose
To disinherit you –

BONARIO   How!

MOSCA   And thrust you forth
As a mere stranger to his blood; 'tis true, sir.   45
The work no way engageth me, but as

49–50 **for which mere respect ... done it**   for which reason, and with no other
motive, I have told you. Mosca pretends to be interested in virtue yet we
are aware that all of his actions stem from a desire to exploit others.

53 **lend it any thought**   give it any credence.

56 **piety**   filial loyalty.

I claim an interest in the general state
Of goodness and true virtue, which I hear
T'abound in you; and, for which mere respect,
Without a second aim, sir, I have done it.   50

BONARIO

This tale hath lost thee much of the late trust
Thou hadst with me; it is impossible –
I know not how to lend it any thought,
My father should be so unnatural.

MOSCA

It is a confidence that well becomes   55
Your piety; and formed, no doubt, it is
From your own simple innocence – which makes
Your wrong more monstrous and abhorred. But, sir,
I now will tell you more. This very minute,
It is, or will be doing; and if you   60
Shall be but pleased to go with me, I'll bring you,
I dare not say where you shall see, but where
Your ear shall be a witness of the deed;
Hear yourself written bastard, and professed
The common issue of the earth.

BONARIO   I'm mazed!   65

MOSCA

Sir, if I do it not, draw your just sword,
And score your vengeance on my front and face;
Mark me your villain. You have too much wrong,
And I do suffer for you, sir. My heart
Weeps blood, in anguish –

BONARIO   Lead. I follow thee.   70

Exeunt

 5 **delicates**   entertainments.
15 **feat body of mine**   nimble, dainty – he is a dwarf.
16 **your bulks**   your larger servants.

Scene three

VOLPONE'S *House*
Enter VOLPONE, *followed by* NANO, ANDROGYNO *and* CASTRONE
VOLPONE

Mosca stays long, methinks. Bring forth your sports
And help to make the wretched time more sweet.

NANO

Dwarf, fool, and eunuch, well met here we be.
A question it were now, whether of us three –
Being, all, the known delicates of a rich man –   5
In pleasing him, claim the precedency can?

CASTRONE I claim for myself.

ANDROGYNO   And so doth the fool.

NANO

'Tis foolish indeed; let me set you both to school.
First, for your dwarf, he's little, and witty,
And every thing, as it is little, is pretty;   10
Else, why do men say to a creature of my shape,
So soon as they see him, 'It's a pretty little ape?'
And, why a pretty ape? but for pleasing imitation
Of greater men's action, in a ridiculous fashion.
Beside, this feat body of mine doth not crave   15
Half the meat, drink, and cloth, one of your bulks will
have.
Admit, your fool's face be the mother of laughter,
Yet, for his brain, it must always come after;
And though that do feed him, it's a pitiful case
His body is beholding to such a bad face.   20

One knocks

VOLPONE

Who's there? my couch; away, look, Nano, see;
Give me my caps, first – go, enquire.

Exeunt NANO, ANDROGYNO, CASTRONE

Now, Cupid

Send it be Mosca, and with fair return.

26 **dwell**   hang around.

27 **that my fit were past**   i.e. so I can get her visit over with.

28–9 **A second hell ... other**   Volpone fears that the purgatory of Lady Would-be's visit, and the hatred he feels for her, will affect his lust for Celia. The scene which follows is an interesting one because it shows Volpone in a trap of his own making (he cannot escape because of his guise of being an invalid) and so foreshadows his later ensnarement by Mosca.

2 **This band**   this collar – her lack of modesty shows she is bent on seduction.

7–8 **these petulant ... done this**   she is referring to the poor workmanship of her servants in making her look beautiful – we, of course, already know from Mosca that they have little to work with.

14 **your fellow**   your fellow servant.

NANO (*At the entrance*)

    It is the beauteous Madam –

VOLPONE   Would-be – is it?

NANO

    The same.

VOLPONE   Now, torment on me; squire her in –   25

    For she will enter, or dwell here for ever.

    Nay, quickly, that my fit were past, (*Exit* NANO) I fear

    A second hell too, that my loathing this

    Will quite expel my appetite to the other.

    Would she were taking, now, her tedious leave.   30

    Lord, how it threats me, what I am to suffer!

Scene four

Enter NANO *with* LADY WOULD-BE

LADY WOULD-BE

    I thank you, good sir. Pray you signify

    Unto your patron, I am here. This band

    Shows not my neck enough – I trouble you, sir,

    Let me request you, bid one of my women

    Come hither to me – in good faith, I am dressed   5

    Most favourably today. It is no matter,

    'Tis well enough. Look, see, these petulant things!

    How they have done this!

VOLPONE (*Aside*)   I do feel the fever

    Ent'ring in at mine ears. O, for a charm,

    To fright it hence.

Enter 1st WOMAN

LADY WOULD-BE   Come nearer. Is this curl   10

    In his right place? or this? why is this higher

    Than all the rest? you ha' not washed your eyes yet?

    Or do they not stand even i' your head?

    Where's your fellow? call her.

                                      Exit 1st WOMAN

18 **forsooth** the servant has mimicked Lady Would-be's rebuke. In reply she can do nothing more than mimic the mimicking. She is a woman without an original idea in her head, as the scene which follows shows.

23–5 **I, that have … every grace** like Volpone when describing his gold, she uses religious terminology to describe her own appearance. The blasphemy is again used to show the moral shallowness of those in Venice.

37 **This fucus** make-up.

NANO (*Aside*)   Now, St Mark
  Deliver us! Anon, she'll beat her women   15
  Because her nose is red.
Enter 1st *and* 2nd WOMEN
LADY OULD-BE   I pray you, view
  This tire, forsooth – are all things apt, or no?
2nd WOMAN
  One hair a little, here, sticks out, forsooth.
LADY WOULD-BE
  Does't so, forsooth? and where was your dear sight
  When it did so, forsooth? what now? bird-eyed?   20
  And you, too? pray you both approach, and mend it.
  Now, by that light, I muse you're not ashamed!
  I, that have preached these things, so oft, unto you,
  Read you the principles, argued all the grounds,
  Disputed every fitness, every grace,   25
  Called you to counsel of so frequent dressings –
NANO (*Aside*)
  More carefully than of your fame or honour.
LADY WOULD-BE
  Made you acquainted, what an ample dowry
  The knowledge of these things would be unto you,
  Able, alone, to get you noble husbands   30
  At your return; and you, thus, to neglect it?
  Besides, you seeing what a curious nation
  Th'Italians are, what will they say of me?
  'The English lady cannot dress herself' –
  Here's a fine imputation to our country!   35
  Well, go your ways, and stay i' the next room.
  This fucus was too coarse too; it's no matter.
  Good sir, you'll give 'em entertainment?
                        Exeunt NANO *and* WOMEN
VOLPONE (*Aside*)
  The storm comes tòward me.
LADY WOULD-BE   How does my Volp?

41 **s*trange fury*** in mythological writing, the Furies were snake-haired goddesses of vengeance who pursued unpunished criminals. Volpone means it as an insult but it completely goes over her head.

47 **the golden mediocrity** she gets her words wrong as she is referring to Aristotle's 'golden mean', a theory of moderation. It is difficult to see where she is going with this – when forced to improvise, she is capable of only nonsense.

51 **passion of the heart** heartburn.

52 **Seed-pearl** a solution believed to be good for ailments of the heart.

53–4 **Tincture of gold ... myrobalans** all were thought to have medicinal properties. Gold was regarded as a stimulant; coral dispelled bad dreams; elecampane was the root of a flowering plant believed to cure stomach disorders; myrobalans, a dried plum-like fruit, used then to cure melancholy, now for dyeing or tanning.

55 **ta'en a grasshopper ... wing** Volpone refers to a proverb which means that it is better to leave nuisances alone. The image is fitting because Lady Would-be flits from one subject to another.

56 **Burnt silk ... muscadel** the list of quack cures continues unabated.

57 **You will not ... part?** Volpone's hint backfires as she believes he is terrified she will leave him.

61 **Bugloss** herb used as a stimulant.

She's in again she's off again.

VOLPONE

    Troubled with noise, I cannot sleep; I dreamt   40

    That a strange fury entered, now, my house,

    And, with the dreadful tempest of her breath,

    Did cleave my roof asunder.

LADY WOULD-BE   Believe me, and I

    Had the most fearful dream, could I remember't –

VOLPONE (*Aside*)

    Out on my fate; I ha' given her the occasion   45

    How to torment me – she will tell me hers.

LADY WOULD-BE

    Methought the golden mediocrity,

    Polite, and delicate –

VOLPONE   O, if you do love me,

    No more; I sweat and suffer at the mention

    Of any dream – feel how I tremble yet.   50

LADY WOULD-BE

    Alas, good soul! the passion of the heart.

    Seed-pearl were good now, boiled with syrup of apples,

    Tincture of gold, and coral, citron-pills,

    Your elecampane root, myrobalans –

VOLPONE (*Aside*)

    Ay me, I have ta'en a grasshopper by the wing.   55

LADY WOULD-BE

    Burnt silk, and amber; you have muscadel

    Good i' the house –

VOLPONE   You will not drink, and part?

LADY WOULD-BE

    No, fear not that. I doubt we shall not get

    Some English saffron – half a dram would serve –

    Your sixteen cloves, a little musk, dried mints,   60

    Bugloss, and barley-meal –

VOLPONE (*Aside*)   She's in again;

    Before I feigned diseases, now I have one.

LADY WOULD-BE

    And these applied, with a right scarlet cloth –

72–3 **Plato ... Pythagoras**   Plato, a Greek philosopher, is regarded as the initiator of western philosophy. He believed in the value of music to education. Pythagoras discovered the numerical ratios defining the intervals of the musical scale (see note to Act 1, scene 2, line 27). Lady Would-be appears to understand neither; she has merely heard of them and is name-dropping.

74 *concent*   harmony.

76 **The poet**   Sophocles, a famous Athenian dramatist and tragic poet.

79 – 81 **Petrarch? ... Cieco di Hadria?**   all are great Italian Renaissance poets.

82 **Is everything ... destruction?**   Volpone is despairing of finding a way of getting rid of her as every word he says seems to lead her down a different avenue.

86 **Pastor Fido**   a pastoral play by Guarini.

VOLPONE (*Aside*)
    Another flood of words! a very torrent!
LADY WOULD-BE
    Shall I, sir, make you a poultice?
VOLPONE   No, no, no;   65
    I'm very well, you need prescribe no more.
LADY WOULD-BE
    I have, a little, studied physic; but now
    I'm all for music – save, i' the forenoons,
    An hour or two for painting. I would have
    A lady, indeed, t'have all letters and arts.   70
    Be able to discourse, to write, to paint,
    But principal (as Plato holds) your music
    (And so does wise Pythagoras, I take it)
    Is your true rapture – when there is concent
    In face, in voice, and clothes – and is, indeed,   75
    Our sex's chiefest ornament.
VOLPONE   The poet
    As old in time as Plato, and as knowing,
    Says that your highest female grace is silence.
LADY WOULD-BE
    Which o' your poets? Petrarch? or Tasso? or Dante?
    Guarini? Ariosto? Aretine?   80
    Cieco di Hadria? I have read them all.
VOLPONE (*Aside*)
    Is everything a cause to my destruction?
LADY WOULD-BE
    I think I ha' two or three of 'em about me.
VOLPONE
    The sun, the sea will sooner, both, stand still
    Than her eternal tongue! nothing can scape it.   85
LADY WOULD-BE
    Here's *Pastor Fido* –
VOLPONE (*Aside*)   Profess obstinate silence,
    That's now my safest.
LADY WOULD-BE   All our English writers,

90 **Montagnié**   sixteenth-century French writer much quoted by English writers.

91 **modern and facile**   both fashionable and easily understood – Lady W's meaning; trivial and superficial – Jonson's intended criticism.

93 **Petrarch**   fourteenth-century Italian love poet especially famous for his sonnets.

94 **trusted 'em with much**   gave much which could be imitated.

95 **Dante**   thirteenth-century Italian poet who wrote *La Divina Commedia*.

96 **Aretine**   sixteenth-century Italian satirist, famous for scurrilous attacks upon leading political figures.

107 **Settling ... subsiding**   the images are chemical ones and are used to suggest that Volpone, by thinking too much about his illness ('settling and fixing') is in danger of becoming listless and deteriorating ('subsiding').

110 **some certain faeces**   some waste products which obstruct our systems and so kill us.

114 **lusty**   she means merry. The irony is that he did feel 'lusty' until she arrived.

I mean such as are happy in th'Italian,
Will deign to steal out of this author, mainly,
Almost as much as from Montagnié –   90
He has so modern and facile a vein,
Fitting the time, and catching the court-ear.
Your Petrarch is more passionate, yet he,
In days of sonneting, trusted 'em with much:
Dante is hard, and few can understand him.   95
But for a desperate wit, there's Aretine!
Only, his pictures are a little obscene –
You mark me not?

VOLPONE   Alas, my mind's perturbed.

LADY WOULD-BE
Why, in such cases, we must cure ourselves,
Make use of our philosophy –

VOLPONE   O'y me!   100

LADY WOULD-BE
And, as we find our passions do rebel,
Encounter 'em with reason; or divert 'em,
By giving scope unto some other humour
Of lesser danger – as in politic bodies,
There's nothing more doth overwhelm the judgment,   105
And clouds the understanding, than too much
Settling, and fixing, and (as't were) subsiding
Upon one object. For the incorporating
Of these same outward things into that part
Which we call mental, leaves some certain faeces   110
That stop the organs, and, as Plato says,
Assassinates our knowledge.

VOLPONE (*Aside*)   Now the spirit
Of patience help me!

LADY WOULD-BE   Come, in faith, I must
Visit you more a-days, and make you well.
Laugh, and be lusty.

VOLPONE (*Aside*)   My good angel save me!   115

120 **As he would ... purpose**   she believes he was too fascinated by her to listen attentively; the truth would be that, paralysed by boredom, he had simply switched off.

125 **cocetanei**   of the same age.

5–7 **The bells ... near it**   Volpone compares her unceasing prattle to the bells which were rung to announce another funeral service for a plague victim and to the betting at a cock-fight.

9–10 **A lawyer ... woman**   two of Jonson's favourite targets are attacked here – both are associated with being garrulous.

LADY WOULD-BE

There was but one sole man, in all the world,
With whom I ere could sympathise; and he
Would lie you often, three, four hours together,
To hear me speak; and be sometime so rapt,
As he would answer me quite from the purpose,   120
Like you, and you are like him, just. I'll discourse –
And't be but only, sir, to bring you asleep –
How we did spend our time, and loves, together,
For some six years.

VOLPONE   Oh, oh, oh, oh, oh, oh.

LADY WOULD-BE

For we were *coætanei*, and brought up –   125

VOLPONE (*Aside*)

Some power, some fate, some fortune rescue me!

Scene five

Enter MOSCA

MOSCA

God save you, madam.

LADY WOULD-BE   Good sir.

VOLPONE   Mosca! welcome,
Welcome to my redemption!

MOSCA   Why, sir?

VOLPONE   Oh,
Rid me of this my torture quickly, there;
My madam with the everlasting voice;
The bells in time of pestilence ne'er made   5
Like noise, or were in that perpetual motion;
The cock-pit comes not near it. All my house,
But now, steamed like a bath with her thick breath.
A lawyer could not have been heard; nor scarce
Another woman, such a hail of words   10
She has let fall. For hell's sake, rid her hence.

12 *presented* given her gift.
23 *they that ... licence* they that appear most wanton.
27 *a paroxysm* a relapse.

MOSCA

   Has she presented?

VOLPONE   O, I do not care,

   I'll take her absence upon any price,

   With any loss.

MOSCA   Madam –

LADY WOULD-BE   I ha' brought your patron

   A toy, a cap here, of mine own work –

MOSCA   'Tis well.   15

   I had forgot to tell you, I saw your knight

   Where you'd little think it –

LADY WOULD-BE   Where?

MOSCA   Marry,

   Where yet, if you make haste, you may apprehend him,

   Rowing upon the water in a gondola,

   With the most cunning courtesan of Venice.   20

LADY WOULD-BE

   Is't true?

MOSCA   Pursue 'em, and believe your eyes –

   Leave me to make your gift. (*Exit* LADY WOULD-BE) I

      knew 'twould take.

   For lightly, they that use themselves most licence

   Are still most jealous.

VOLPONE   Mosca, hearty thanks

   For thy quick fiction and delivery of me.   25

   Now, to my hopes, what say'st thou?

Re-enter LADY WOULD-BE

LADY WOULD-BE   But do you hear,

     sir? –

VOLPONE

   Again: I fear a paroxysm.

LADY WOULD-BE   Which way

   Rowed they together?

MOSCA   Toward the *Rialto*.

36 **wanton gamester at primero**   like a reckless gambler in a card game. What
follows are all terms from the game of primero, used as sexual
euphemisms by Volpone. To 'go less' is to wager a small stake, a thing he
has no intention of doing as he will stake all to get Celia. 'To lie' is to place
a bet, to 'draw' is to take another card; he will lie where he is, draw Celia
to him and have sexual intercourse with her.

2 **send**   send for you. Mosca is horrified to see Corvino at the door because it
upsets his plans and means that he now has three masks to wear: one to
Corbaccio, another to Bonario, a third to Corvino.

LADY WOULD-BE

    I pray you, lend me your dwarf.

MOSCA   I pray you, take him.

                                 (*Exit* LADY WOULD-BE)

    Your hopes, sir, are like happy blossoms, fair,   30

    And promise timely fruit, if you will stay

    But the maturing; keep you at your couch –

    Corbaccio will arrive straight, with the will;

    When he is gone, I'll tell you more.

                                            Exit

VOLPONE   My blood,

    My spirits are returned; I am alive;   35

    And like your wanton gamester at primero,

    Whose thought had whispered to him, not go less,

    Methinks I lie, and draw – for an encounter.

Scene six

Enter MOSCA, BONARIO

MOSCA

    Sir, here concealed, you may hear all. But pray you

    Have patience, sir; (*One knocks*) the same's your father

      knocks;

    I am compelled to leave you.

BONARIO   Do so. Yet

    Cannot my thought imagine this a truth.

                                   Hides himself

Scene seven

Enter CORVINO, CELIA

MOSCA

    Death on me! you are come too soon, what meant you?

    Did not I say I would send?

3 **prevent us**   i.e. from getting my legacy.

4–5 **Did e'er ... place**   did ever a man rush so to be cuckolded? A courtier
      would not be so impatient when trying for a place at court. It is a
      common device that Mosca's asides, whilst intended to be the
      externalising of his personal glee, serve almost as a direct commentary for
      the audience. They add much humour to the play.

9 **except you told me**   except for what you have told me.

22 **I would avoid ... tricks**   I want to avoid all tricks and stratagems.

24 **Affect not ... trials**   do not pretend to be tempting my constancy again.
      Celia cannot believe her husband to be capable of so gross a suggestion
      so sees it as yet another test of her.

CORVINO   Yes, but I feared
  You might forget it, and then they prevent us.
MOSCA
  Prevent? (*Aside*) – Did e'er man haste so for his horns?
  A courtier would not ply it so, for a place. –   5
  Well, now there's no helping it, stay here;
  I'll presently return.

                                    Moves toward BONARIO
CORVINO   Where are you, Celia?
  You know not wherefore I have brought you hither?
CELIA
  Not well, except you told me.
CORVINO   Now I will;
  Hark hither.

                                    They whisper apart
MOSCA (*To* BONARIO)   Sir, your father hath sent word   10
  It will be half an hour ere he come;
  And therefore, if you please to walk the while
  Into that gallery – at the upper end
  There are some books to entertain the time;
  And I'll take care, no man shall come unto you, sir.   15
BONARIO
  Yes, I will stay there. (*Aside*) I do doubt this fellow.

                                                  Exit

MOSCA
  There, he is far enough; he can hear nothing;
  And for his father, I can keep him off.

                                    Moves to VOLPONE
CORVINO
  Nay, now, there is no starting back; and therefore
  Resolve upon it; I have so decreed.   20
  It must be done. Nor would I move't afore,
  Because I would avoid all shifts and tricks
  That might deny me.
CELIA   Sir, let me beseech you,
  Affect not these strange trials; if you doubt

27 **Where I may please your fears** where I can put your fears to rest.

28 **I have no such humour** I have no jealousy.

30 **Not horn-mad** not mad enough to risk being cuckolded; mad at the thought of being cuckolded.

32 **train** trap.

34 **engagements** my previous commitments i.e. how much I have already given.

37 **respect my venture** support my plan.

38 **Before your ... breath** Celia is amazed that Corvino would put money before his honour. Her husband dismisses her moral scruples contemptuously: he sees honour, which he has earlier made much of, as being trivial compared to gold. He deserves his fate because he seeks it so vigorously.

43–4 **takes his meat ... fingers** i.e. is fed by someone else.

45 **When you do scald his gums** i.e. he is too weak to cry out when the meat is too hot.

  a shadow his description of Volpone shows his blindness to truth.

46–7 **what spirit ... entered him?** what evil spirit has possessed him?

47 **fame** reputation.

48 **such a jig** so trivial.

51 **Whose lips are i' my pocket** i.e. I have power over him because I will soon own him.

My chastity, why, lock me up, for ever!   25
Make me the heir of darkness. Let me live
Where I may please your fears, if not your trust.

CORVINO

Believe it, I have no such humour, I.
All that I speak I mean; yet I am not mad –
Not horn-mad, see you? Go to, show yourself   30
Obedient, and a wife.

CELIA   O heaven!

CORVINO   I say it,
Do so.

CELIA   Was this the train?

CORVINO   I've told you reasons;
What the physicians have set down; how much
It may concern me; what my engagements are;
My means; and the necessity of those means   35
For my recovery; wherefore, if you be
Loyal, and mine, be won, respect my venture.

CELIA

Before your honour?

CORVINO   Honour? tut, a breath;
There's no such thing in nature – a mere term
Invented to awe fools. What is my gold   40
The worse, for touching? clothes, for being looked on?
Why, this's no more. An old, decrepit wretch,
That has no sense, no sinew; takes his meat
With others' fingers; only knows to gape
When you do scald his gums; a voice; a shadow;   45
And what can this man hurt you?

CELIA   Lord! what spirit
Is this hath entered him?

CORVINO   And for your fame,
That's such a jig; as if I would go tell it,
Cry it, on the Piazza! who shall know it,
But he, that cannot speak it, and this fellow,   50
Whose lips are i' my pocket – save yourself?

60   **Aretine**   poet who provided the commentary for a set of erotic drawings by
        Guilio Romano. See also note to Act 3, scene 4, line 96.

62   **professed critic in lechery**   self-confessed expert in lechery.

66   **honest polity ... own**   a sound scheme to assure me of inheriting the wealth.

If you'll proclaim't, you may. I know no other
Should come to know it.

CELIA   Are heaven and saints then
   nothing?
Will they be blind, or stupid?

CORVINO   How?

CELIA   Good sir,
Be jealous still, emulate them; and think   55
What hate they burn with tòward every sin.

CORVINO
I grant you, if I thought it were a sin,
I would not urge you. Should I offer this
To some young Frenchman, or hot Tuscan blood,
That had read Aretine, conned all his prints,   60
Knew every quirk within lust's labyrinth,
And were professed critic in lechery –
And I would look upon him, and applaud him,
This were a sin. But here, 'tis contrary,
A pious work, mere charity, for p'hysic,   65
And honest polity to assure mine own.

CELIA
O heaven! canst thou suffer such a change?

VOLPONE
Thou art mine honour, Mosca, and my pride,
My joy, my tickling, my delight! go, bring 'em.

MOSCA (*Advancing*)
Please you draw near, sir.

CORVINO   Come on, what –   70
You will not be rebellious? by that light –

                     Drags her towards the bed

MOSCA
Sir, Signior Corvino, here, is come to see you –

VOLPONE
Oh!

MOSCA   And hearing of the consultation had

74 **to prostitute** Corvino takes Mosca to mean that he is offering a sacrifice, such is his blindness to the way he is being conned. Mosca, in supreme control, cannot resist being malicious.

84–5 **Applying fire ... grow again** Volpone protests his impotence using natural images.

97–9 **Cry thee ... raw rochet** again we see a mind twisted by greed. He begins by saying that unless she will sleep with Volpone, he will denounce her publicly as a harlot; paradoxically, he has already promised that he will denounce her if she does agree to prostitute herself. He goes on to threaten her again with dissection, this time in the most brutal terms.

So lately for your health, is come to offer,
Or rather, sir, to prostitute –

CORVINO   Thanks, sweet Mosca.   75

MOSCA

Freely, unasked, or unentreated –

CORVINO   Well.

MOSCA

As the true, fervent instance of his love,
His own most fair and proper wife, the beauty
Only of price in Venice –

CORVINO   'Tis well urged.

MOSCA

To be your comfortress, and to preserve you.   80

VOLPONE

Alas, I'm past already! pray you, thank him
For his good care, and promptness; but for that,
'Tis a vain labour; e'en to fight 'gainst heaven;
Applying fire to a stone – uh, uh, uh, uh –
Making a dead leaf grow again. I take   85
His wishes gently, though; and you may tell him
What I've done for him. Marry, my state is hopeless!
Will him to pray for me, and t'use his fortune
With reverence, when he comes to't.

MOSCA   Do you hear, sir?
Go to him, with your wife.

CORVINO   Heart of my father!   90
Wilt thou persist thus? come, I pray thee, come.
Thou seest 'tis nothing. Celia! By this hand,
I shall grow violent. Come, do't, I say.

CELIA

Sir, kill me, rather. I will take down poison,
Eat burning coals, do anything –

CORVINO   Be damned!   95
Heart, I will drag thee hence, home, by the hair;
Cry thee a strumpet through the streets; rip up
Thy mouth, unto thine ears; and slit thy nose,

100–6 **I will buy . . . I'll do't**   Corvino's fury leads him into making even more vile threats. He now threatens to murder a slave, tie the dead Celia to him and then put them on public display, having first burned her supposed crime of adultery into her skin with acid. All this because she refuses to sleep with another man!

109 **Think who it is entreats you**   having threatened her, he now appeals to her wifely sense of duty. He is blind to the irony of this plea.

114 **Will you . . . undoing?**   a heavily ironic line – Celia, by her resistance, is trying to avoid doing these very things.

116 **She has watched her time**   she has waited for this opportunity.

119 **Crocodile**   he believes her tears are fake. This is one occasion when the animal imagery says more about the speaker than it does about the person described.

Like a raw rochet – Do not tempt me, come.
Yield I am loath – Death, I will buy some slave,   100
Whom I will kill, and bind thee to him, alive;
And at my window, hang you forth – devising
Some monstrous crime, which I, in capital letters,
Will eat into thy flesh, with aquafortis
And burning corsives, on this stubborn breast.   105
Now, by the blood thou hast incensed, I'll do't.

CELIA

Sir, what you please, you may; I am your martyr.

CORVINO

Be not thus obstinate, I ha' not deserved it.
Think who it is entreats you. Pray thee, sweet;
Good faith, thou shalt have jewels, gowns, attires,   110
What thou wilt think, and ask – Do, but go kiss him.
Or touch him, but. For my sake. At my suit.
This once, No? not? I shall remember this.
Will you disgrace me thus? do you thirst my undoing?

MOSCA

Nay, gentle lady, be advised.

CORVINO   No. no.   115
She has watched her time. God's precious, this is
    scurvy;
'Tis very scurvy; and you are –

MOSCA   Nay, good sir.

CORVINO

An arrant locust, by heaven, a locust. Whore,
Crocodile, that hast thy tears prepared,
Expecting how thou'lt bid 'em flow.

MOSCA   Nay, pray you, sir,   120
She will consider.

CELIA   Would my life would serve
To satisfy –

CORVINO   'Sdeath, if she would but speak to him,
And save my reputation, 'twere somewhat;
But spitefully to affect my utter ruin!

126 *quit* excuse; let her off.

127 *coming* forthcoming.

133–8 *O God ... for money?* Celia's prayer is both touching and a damning condemnation of the morality of the day. She despairs that honour, which was once man's main motive for living, should now be deemed less precious than gold; a trifle to be shaken off when it is inconvenient to uphold.

139 *Ay, in Corvino ... minds* Volpone, ironically, agrees with her as he begins his attempt at seduction.

144 *a cope-man* a merchant.

148 *shapes* disguises.

151 *I would have ... love* I would have abandoned all of my schemes for your love.

MOSCA

   Ay, now you've put your fortune in her hands.   125
   Why i'faith, it is her modesty, I must quit her;
   If you were absent, she would be more coming;
   I know it, and dare undertake for her.
   What woman can, before her husband? Pray you,
   Let us depart, and leave her here.

CORVINO   Sweet Celia,   130
   Thou mayst redeem all yet; I'll say no more.
   If not, esteem yourself as lost. (CELIA *starts to leave*) Nay,
     stay there.

                              Exeunt CORVINO, MOSCA

CELIA

   O God, and his good angels! whither, whither
   Is shame fled human breasts? that with such ease
   Men dare put off your honours, and their own?   135
   Is that, which ever was a cause of life,
   Now placed beneath the basest circumstance?
   And modestly an exile made, for money?

VOLPONE

   Ay, in Corvino, and such earth-fed minds,
                          (*He leaps off from his couch*)
   That never tasted the true heaven of love.   140
   Assure thee, Celia, he that would sell thee,
   Only for hope of gain, and that uncertain,
   He would have sold his part of paradise
   For ready money, had he met a cope-man.
   Why art thou mazed to see me thus revived?   145
   Rather applaud thy beauty's miracle;
   'Tis thy great work, that hath, not now alone,
   But sundry times raised me, in several shapes,
   And but this morning like a mountebank,
   To see thee at thy window. Ay, before   150
   I would have left my practice for thy love,
   In varying figures I would have contended

153 **Proteus**   a sea god who changed his shape continually.

the hornèd flood   a river god, Achelous, changed his shape to a bull to fight Hercules.

158 **as jovial plight**   happy condition. However, the reference to Jove, father of the gods, is by no means accidental, considering his earlier claims of love. He is saying that she makes him feel divine. Ironically, Jove undertook different shapes, usually to ravish young girls; the most notable of these was Leda whom he raped in the guise of a swan.

161 **the great Valois**   Henry, duke of Anjou and later king of France, was entertained in Venice in 1574.

162 **Antinous**   a beautiful young man, favoured by Emperor Hadrian.

166–83 **Song**   the beauty of the song contrasts with his motives for singing it. It would be easy for the audience to be fooled by Volpone's act here but later we will hear him say that he enjoyed his victory at the subsequent court case as much as if he had 'had the wench'.

With the blue Proteus, or the hornèd flood.
Now, art thou welcome.
CELIA   Sir!
VOLPONE   Nay, fly me not.
Nor, let thy false imagination   155
That I was bed-rid, make thee think I am so;
Thou shalt not find it. I am now as fresh,
As hot, as high, and in as jovial plight,
As when – in that so celebrated scene
At recitation of our comedy   160
For entertainment of the great Valois –
I acted young Antinous; and attracted
The eyes and ears of all the ladies present,
T'admire each graceful gesture, note, and footing.

Song   165

Come, my Celia, let us prove,
While we can, the sports of love;
Time will not be ours for ever,
He, at length, our good will sever;
Spend not then his gifts in vain.   170
Suns that set may rise again;
But if, once, we lose this light,
'Tis with us perpetual night.
Why should we defer our joys?
Fame and rumour are but toys.   175
Cannot we delude the eyes
Of a few poor household spies?
Or his easier ears beguile,
Thus removèd, by our wile?
'Tis no sin, love's fruits to steal,   180
But the sweet thefts to reveal;
To be taken, to be seen,
These have crimes accounted been.

184 **sèrene** poisonous disease.

190 **feed others** Volpone is apparently playing a dangerous game by revealing so much until one realises that he cannot lose. If Celia gives in, who can she tell of what she has learned without destroying her own reputation?

192 **Egyptian queen** Cleopatra was reputed to have dissolved an expensive pearl in vinegar and then drunk it to impress Antony of her wealth.

193–4 **a carbuncle ... St Mark** the reference is to a large jewel but the image remains unclear.

195 **Lollia Paulina** Caligula's wife, famed for her horde of jewels.

200 **private patrimony** the endowment of a church – Volpone boasts they will eat its worth in one meal. Again he equates riches with food.

202–5 **The heads of ... our dish** the dishes described substitute exotic birds for plainer meats, finishing with the mythical phoenix, which he would consume even if it meant condemning the bird to extinction.

207–10 **but I ... sensual baits** unlike others in Venice, Celia remains unmoved in the face of such promised sensual pleasures, recognising them as traps both in spiritual and literal terms. For her, innocence is the only treasure worth keeping. Such virtue is admirable, all the more so because it is absent elsewhere.

211 **beggar's virtue** for Volpone, conscience is merely a route to poverty.

215 **milk of unicorns** an exotic boast indeed, as the creature was mythical. Our distaste at his intent should not blind us to the beauty of the images he uses to tempt her with a life of opulence.

CELIA
  Some serene blast me, or dire lightning strike
  This my offending race.
VOLPONE   Why droops my Celia?   185
  Thou hast in place of a base husband found
  A worthy lover; use thy fortune well,
  With secrecy, and pleasure. See, behold,
  What thou art queen of; not in expectation,
  As I feed others, but possessed, and crowned.   190
  See, here, a rope of pearl, and each more orient
  Than that the brave Egyptian queen caroused;
  Dissolve, and drink 'em. See, a carbuncle,
  May put out both the eyes of our St Mark;
  A diamond, would have bought Lollia Paulina,   195
  When she came in like star-light, hid with jewels
  That were the spoils of provinces; take these,
  And wear, and lose 'em; yet remains an ear-ring
  To purchase them again, and this whole state.
  A gem but worth a private patrimony   200
  Is nothing – we will eat such at a meal.
  The heads of parrots, tongues of nightingales,
  The brains of peacocks, and of ostriches
  Shall be our food; and, could we get the phoenix,
  Though nature lost her kind, she were our dish.   205
CELIA
  Good sir, these things might move a mind affected
  With such delights; but I, whose innocence
  Is all I can think wealthy, or worth th'enjoying,
  And which once lost, I have naught to lose beyond it,
  Cannot be taken with these sensual baits.   210
  If you have conscience –
VOLPONE   'Tis the beggar's virtue;
  If thou hast wisdom, hear me, Celia.
  Thy baths shall be the juice of Jùly-flowers,
  Spirit of roses, and of violets,
  The milk of unicorns, and panthers' breath   215

219 *vertigo* dizziness.

221 *changèd shapes ... tales* his final temptation is related to Ovid's work, *Metamorphoses*, which details the many transformations the Greek gods undertook in order to seduce. Volpone promises that they will act out these stories in their love-making.

222 *Europa ... Jove* Jove abducted Europa disguised as a bull, whilst still married to Juno.

223 *Mars ... Erycine* Mars was caught in an adulterous affair with Venus (Erycine) by her husband, Vulcan.

226–30 *Then will ... mistress* having exhausted all of these roles they will enact scenes from more modern times. She will be seduced in the guise of the wife of great rulers.

234 *transfuse* suck our souls into each other's body.

240–59 *If you have ... your health* Celia's plea is all the more touching because of its broken rhythm, which conveys her distress and fear. However, one cannot help feeling her response is a little melodramatic.

Gathered in bags, and mixed with Cretan wines.
Our drink shall be preparèd gold and amber;
Which we will take, until my roof whirl round
With the vertigo; and dwarf shall dance,
My eunuch sing, my fool make up the antic.   220
Whilst we, changèd shapes, act Ovid's tales,
Thou like Europa now, and I like Jove,
Then I like Mars, and thou like Erycine,
So of the rest, till we have quite run through
And wearied all the fables of the gods.   225
Then will I have thee in more modern forms,
Attirèd like some sprightly dame of France,
Brave Tuscan lady, or proud Spanish beauty;
Sometimes unto the Persian Sophy's wife;
Or the Grand Signior's mistress; and, for change,   230
To one of our most artful courtesans,
Or some quick Negro, or cold Russian;
And I will meet thee in as many shapes;
Where we may, so, transfuse our wand'ring souls,
Out at our lips, and score up sums of pleasures,   235

                                                            (*Sings*)

        That the curious shall not know
        How to tell them as they flow;
        And the envious, when they find
        What their number is, be pined.

CELIA (*Haltingly*)
If you have ears that will be pierced ... or eyes   240
That can be opened ... a heart, may be touched ...
Or any part that yet sounds man about you ...
If you have touch of holy saints ... or heaven ...
Do me the grace to let me scape ... If not,
Be bountiful, and kill me ... You do know   245
I am a creature hither ill betrayed

                                                              167

249 **Yet feed ... lust ...** her view coloured by life with Corvino, she sees anger and lust as interchangeable. The description which follows is reminiscent of his earlier threats to her. She blames herself for the situation, a sure sign that she is terrified. Sadly, she is appealing to a virtue which simply does not exist.

257 **disfavour me** disfigure me.

260 **Think me cold** there is an irony here, in that he means passionless whilst, for a brief moment, she will think he is referring to a sense of mercy. The image becomes all the more cruel because of this.

262 **Nestor's hernia** Nestor was an esteemed king, the oldest to take part in the Trojan Wars. His age was associated with impotence and Juvenal added to this in **The Satires** by describing him as having a hernia.

263 **degenerate ... nation** Volpone has ran out of patience and now claims that if he does not act he will be betraying the reputation of Italians for virility. His lack of feeling is shocking and yet comical, as he attributes Celia's restraint to a tactical error on his part; 'did the deed' contrasts strongly with his earlier protestations of love.

s.d. **Bonario leaps out** his intervention is beautifully timed, in that it is both comic, particularly when one considers the reaction of Volpone to it, and yet a fitting answer to Celia's prayer.

267 **Forbear ... swine!** his opening words add to the comedy because they are so grand and antiquated. He appears almost like a pompous fool.

272 **Before this altar ... idol** Bonario sees the corrupted values of Volpone, guessing correctly that he adores gold as others do God. He dismisses the riches as 'dross'.

By one whose shame I would forget it were . . .
If you will deign me neither of these graces,
Yet feed your wrath, sir, rather than your lust . . .
(It is a vice, comes nearer manliness) . . .   250
And punish that unhappy crime of nature,
Which you miscall my beauty . . . Flay my face,
Or poison it with ointments for seducing
Your blood to this rebellion . . . Rub these hands
With what may cause an eating leprosy,   255
E'en to my bones and marrow . . . anything
That may disfavour me, save in my honour . . .
And I will kneel to you, pray for you, pay down
A thousand hourly vows, sir, for your health . . .
Report, and think you virtuous –

VOLPONE   Think me cold,   260
Frozen, and impotent, and so report me?
That I had Nestor's hernia, thou wouldst think.
I do degenerate, and abuse my nation,
To play with opportunity thus long;
I should have done the act, and then have parleyed.   265
Yield, or I'll force thee.

CELIA   O! just God.

VOLPONE   In vain –

         BONARIO *leaps out from where Mosca had placed him*

BONARIO
Forbear, foul ravisher! libidinous swine!
Free the forced lady, or thou diest, impostor.
But that I am loath to snatch thy punishment
Out of the hand of justice, thou shouldst yet   270
Be made the timely sacrifice of vengeance
Before this altar, and this dross, thy idol.
Lady, let's quit the place, it is the den
Of villainy; fear naught, you have a guard;
And he, ere long, shall meet his just reward.   275

        Exeunt BONARIO, CELIA

276–9 **Fall on me ... ruin** Volpone's response, as in Act 2, scene 5, is
  melodramatic. He falls once more into a despair from which Mosca must
  lift him. Increasingly, he is putting himself into Mosca's power.

  7 **engagèd** at stake.

10 **hearkened** listened in.

12 **expiate the mischance** put right the misfortune.

14 **requite** repay the favour.

  like Romans by committing suicide to avoid dishonour.

15 **like Grecians** libidinously.

VOLPONE

    Fall on me, roof, and bury me in ruin;
    Become my grave, that wert my shelter. O!
    I am unmasked, unspirited, undone,
    Betrayed to beggary, to infamy –

Scene eight

Enter MOSCA, *bleeding*

MOSCA

    Where shall I run, most wretched shame of men,
    To beat out my unlucky brains?

VOLPONE   Here, here.

    What! dost thou bleed?

MOSCA   O, that his well-driven sword
    Had been so courteous to have cleft me down
    Unto the navel, ere I lived to see   5
    My life, my hopes, my spirits, my patron, all
    Thus desperately engagèd, by my error.

VOLPONE

    Woe, on thy fortune.

MOSCA   And my follies, sir.

VOLPONE

    Th'hast made me miserable.

MOSCA   And myself, sir.

    Who would have thought he would have hearkened so?   10

VOLPONE

    What shall we do?

MOSCA   I know not; if my heart
    Could expiate the mischance, I'd pluck it out.
    Will you be pleased to hang me? or cut my throat?
    And I'll requite you, sir. Let's die like Romans,
    Since we have lived like Grecians.

                             They knock without

VOLPONE   Hark, who's there?   15

16 **Saffi** the police.

17 **brand** criminals were branded in order to make their crimes apparent to all.

20–1 **Guilty men ... deserve still** guilty men often fear they are going to be punished when they are not.

8 **This act ... indeed** Corbaccio really intends to disinherit him now, rather than temporarily as before.

I hear some footing – officers, the *Saffi,*
Come to apprehend us! I do feel the brand
Hissing already at my forehead; now
Mine ears are boring.

MOSCA   To your couch, sir; you
Make that place good, however. Guilty men   20
Suspect what they deserve still. Signior Corbaccio!

Scene nine

Enter CORBACCIO

CORBACCIO
Why! how now? Mosca!

Enter VOLTORE *unseen*

MOSCA   O, undone, amazed, sir.
Your son – I know not by what accident –
Acquainted with your purpose to my patron
Touching your will, and making him your heir,
Entered our house with violence, his sword drawn,   5
Sought for you, called you wretch, unnatural,
Vowed he would kill you.

CORBACCIO   Me?

MOSCA   Yes, and my patron.

CORBACCIO
This act shall disinherit him indeed;
Here is the will.

MOSCA   'Tis well, sir.

CORBACCIO   Right and well.
Be you as careful now for me.

MOSCA   My life, sir,   10
Is not more tendered; I am only yours.

CORBACCIO
How does he? will he die shortly, thinkst thou?

MOSCA   I fear
He'll outlast May.

14 *a dram*   Corbaccio is still thinking of poisoning Volpone.

15 *This is a knave, I see*   Volpone now sees Mosca's potential for betrayal for the first time. His accusation is false here, but his premonition will prove to be correct, even if he fails to heed it.

22 *Put not ... upon me*   do not try to deceive me.

CORBACCIO Today?

MOSCA No, last out May, sir.

CORBACCCIO

Couldst thou not gi' him a dram?

MOSCA O, by no means, sir.

CORBACCIO

Nay, I'll not bid you.

Walks aside

VOLTORE (*Aside*) This is a knave, I see. 15

MOSCA (*Aside*)

How! Signior Voltore! did he hear me?

VOLTORE Parasite!

MOSCA

Who's that? O, sir, most timely welcome –

VOLPONE Scarce

To the discovery of your tricks, I fear.

You are his, only? and mine, also? are you not?

MOSCA

Who? I, sir!

VOLTORE You, sir. What device is this 20

About a will?

MOSCA A plot for you, sir.

VOLTORE Come,

Put not your foists upon me, I shall scent 'em.

MOSCA

Did you not hear it?

VOLTORE Yes, I hear Corbaccio

Hath made your patron there his heir.

MOSCA 'Tis true,

By my device, drawn to it by my plot, 25

With hope –

VOLTORE Your patron should reciprocate?

And you have promised?

MOSCA For your good, I did, sir.

Nay more, I told his son, brought, hid him here,

Where he might hear his father pass the deed;

175

32 **_disclaiming_**   disowning in law.

36 **_stated in a double hope_**   Voltore stands to get not only Volpone's fortune but also that bequeathed to the latter by Corbaccio, whom Bonario will have killed in a rage. The plot may be intricate but it is a fitting testament to Mosca's ingenuity.

37 **_Truth be ... conscience_**   the glib reference to these virtues is intentionally blasphemous. Mosca is once more gaining control.

39 **_two old rotten sepulchres_**   Volpone and Corbaccio are pictured as walking tombs.

55 **Scrutineo**   the law court at the Venetian Senate House.

Being persuaded to it by this thought, sir,   30
That the unnaturalness, first, of the act,
And then, his father's oft disclaiming in him –
Which I did mean t'help on – would sure enrage him
To do some violence upon his parent,
On which the law should take sufficient hold,   35
And you be stated in a double hope.
Truth be my comfort, and my conscience,
My only aim was to dig you a fortune
Out of these two, old rotten sepulchres –

VOLTORE

I cry thee mercy, Mosca.

MOSCA   – worth your patience   40
And your great merit, sir. And, see the change!

VOLTORE

Why? what success?

MOSCA   Most hapless! you must help, sir.
Whilst we expected th' old raven, in comes
Corvino's wife, sent hither by her husband –

VOLTORE

What, with a present?

MOSCA   No, sir, on visitation   45
(I'll tell you how anon), and, staying long,
The youth, he grows impatient, rushes forth,
Seizeth the lady, wounds me, makes her swear
(Or he would murder her, that was his vow)
T'affirm my patron to have done her rape;   50
Which how unlike it is, you see! and hence,
With that pretext, he's gone, t'accuse his father,
Defame my patron, defeat you –

VOLTORE   Where's her husband?
Let him be sent for straight.

MOSCA   Sir, I'll go fetch him.

VOLTORE

Bring him to the *Scrutineo*.

MOSCA   Sir, I will.   55

58 **want of counsel**   lack of judgement.

60 **clerks**   scholars.

63 **Need ... labour bless**   Volpone's sardonic response is fittingly irreverent. For him, prayer is to be resorted to only in times of hardship, just as virtue can be traded in times of wealth.

VOLTORE

This must be stopped.

MOSCA   O, you do nobly, sir.

Alas, 'twas laboured all, sir, for your good;

Nor was there any want of counsel in the plot;

But fortune can, at any time, o'erthrow

The projects of a hundred learned clerks, sir.   60

CORBACCIO (*Overhearing*)

What's that?

VOLTORE   Wilt please you, sir, to go along?

Exeunt CORBACCIO, VOLTORE

MOSCA

Patron, go in and pray for our success.

VOLPONE

Need makes devotion; Heaven your labour bless.

Exeunt

179

1–2 **you see … observation is**   you see what you can find out by keeping your eyes open. To give the audience a brief respite from the pace of the main plot, Jonson includes a comic interlude, in which Sir Politic lectures Peregrine on how to behave abroad before revealing some hair-brained money-making schemes.

4 **height** latitude.

6 **this meridian**   with this city in mind.

8–9 **I will not … old** I will not discuss language or dress for these are old subjects. Peregrine deliberately misinterprets this as a personal insult.

10 **themes** subjects.

11 **I'll slander … wit**   either, I won't accredit intelligence to you again; or, I won't think you are exercising your wit at my expense again.

12 **garb** bearing

13 **Very reserved and locked**   i.e. keep your cards close to your chest.

15–16 **make sure … company**   Sir Politic is reminiscent of Polonius in *Hamlet* when giving this fatherly advice; his, however, is largely meaningless. Here he tells him to choose his company with care and then goes on to say that, even with these, never say something that couldn't be denied later.

17 **strangers** foreigners.

20 **So as I … 'em**   in order to keep myself safe from them.

21 **You shall … hourly**   you will constantly be subjected to confidence tricks if you do not.

Act Four

Scene one

A Street
Enter SIR POLITIC WOULD-BE, PEREGRINE
SIR POLITIC

    I told you, sir, it was a plot, you see
    What observation is. You mentioned me
    For some instructions: I will tell you, sir,
    (Since we are met here in this height of Venice)
    Some few particulars I have set down   5
    Only for this meridian; fit to be known
    Of your crude traveller, and they are these.
    I will not touch, sir, at your phrase, or clothes,
    For they are old.
PEREGRINE   Sir, I have better.
SIR POLITIC   Pardon,
    I meant, as they are themes.
PEREGRINE   O, sir, proceed;   10
    I'll slander you no more of wit, good sir.
SIR POLITIC

    First, for your garb, it must be grave and serious;
    Very reserved and locked; not tell a secret
    On any term, not to your father; scarce
    A fable but with caution; make sure choice   15
    Both of your company and discourse; beware
    You never speak a truth –
PEREGRINE   How!
SIR POLITIC   Not to strangers,
    For those be they you must converse with most;
    Others I would not know, sir, but at distance,
    So as I still might be a saver in 'em;   20
    You shall have tricks, else, passed upon you hourly.
    And then, for your religion, profess none,

26–7 **Nick Machiavel ... Bodin**   like his wife, he knows the names of famous
people but not much more. Machiavelli was a great political strategist,
who argued that the end always justified the means where the safety of
the state was involved. He believed religion was a source of potential
division, and thus disruption. Bodin, another political thinker, favoured
religious tolerance and was therefore accused of heresy and atheism.

29 **The metal of your glass**   the quality of your glass (for which Venice was, and
is, famous).

34 **Preposterous**   getting things muddled up.

has him straight   has the measure of him immediately.

39 **And nothing else**   the aside shows that Peregrine believes that the knight has
words but not knowledge; there is no substance to his advice.

40 **Contarini**   a Venetian whose guide to the city had been published in
England.

41 **Dealt with my Jews**   in other words, he borrowed money from Jewish
usurers to pay for his furniture.

46 **projects**   schemes.

But wonder at the diversity of all;
And, for your part, protest, were there no other
But simply the laws o' th' land, you could content you;   25
Nick Machiavel and Monsieur Bodin, both
Were of this mind. Then, must you learn the use
And handling of your silver fork at meals;
The metal of your glass (these are main matters
With your Italian) and to know the hour   30
When you must eat your melons and your figs.

PEREGRINE
Is that a point of state, too?

SIR POLITIC   Here it is.
For your Venetian, if he see a man
Preposterous in the least, he has him straight;
He has, he strips him. I'll acquaint you, sir.   35
I now have lived here . . . 'tis some fourteen months;
Within the first week of my landing here,
All took me for a citizen of Venice,
I knew the forms so well –

PEREGRINE (*Aside*)   And nothing else.

SIR POLITIC
I had read Contarini, took me a house,   40
Dealt with my Jews, to furnish it with movables . . .
Well, if I could but find one man . . . one man
To mine own heart, whom I durst trust . . . I would . . .

PEREGRINE
What? what, sir?

SIR POLITIC   Make him rich; make him a fortune;
He should not think again. I would command it.   45

PEREGRINE
As how?

SIR POLITIC With certain projects that I have,
Which I may not discover.

PEREGRINE (*Aside*)   If I had
But one to wager with, I would lay odds now
He tells me instantly.

183

51 **red herrings**   popular delicacies. However, Venice, being a sea port, was already well provided with all types of fish. His scheme is reminiscent of the saying, 'Taking coals to Newcastle'.

54 **one o' th' States**   a representative of one of the Dutch states.

55 **He cannot ... his mark**   Sir Politic has been pretending that this is a scheme with government approval yet his contact is illiterate.

56 **chandler**   candle-seller. Peregrine means that the paper is greasy.

57 **cheesemonger**   Sir Politic takes him seriously and reveals the occupation of the man who will sell him fish – a cheese merchant!

60 **I've cast it all**   I've planned it all.

   hoy   a small Dutch boat.

63 **save**   break even.

64 **defalk**   can reduce my prices and still make a profit (how is not apparent).

66 **draw the subtle air**   breathe the intrigue-charged air of this city.

72 **cautions**   safeguards, with which he hopes to win a pension from the city fathers.

74–5 **To the Great ... Ten**   Sir Politic envisages himself being passed up the government's hierarchy, as more important officials hear of his schemes.

78 **a commandadore**   a minor official, who Sir Politic thinks hold great sway with the mighty.

SIR POLITIC　　　　　One is (and that
　I care not greatly who knows) to serve the state　　　　50
　Of Venice with red herrings for three years,
　And at a certain rate, from Rotterdam,
　Where I have correspondence. There's a letter,
　Sent me from one o' th' States, and to that purpose;
　He cannot write his name, but that's his mark.　　　　55

PEREGRINE
　He is a chandler?

SIR POLITIC　　　　No, a cheesemonger.
　There are some other too with whom I treat
　About the same negotiation;
　And I will undertake it; for, 'tis thus,
　I'll do't with ease, I've cast it all. Your hoy　　　　60
　Carries but three men in her, and a boy;
　And she shall make me three returns a year;
　So, if there come but one of three, I save,
　If two, I can defalk. But this is now
　If my main project fail.

PEREGRINE　　　　　　Then you have others?　　　　65

SIR POLITIC
　I should be loath to draw the subtle air
　Of such a place without my thousand aims.
　I'll not dissemble, sir; where'er I come
　I love to be considerative; and 'tis true
　I have at my free hours thought upon　　　　70
　Some certain goods unto the state of Venice,
　Which I do call my cautions; and, sir, which
　I mean, in hope of pension, to propound
　To the Great Council, then unto the Forty,
　So to the Ten. My means are made already –　　　　75

PEREGRINE
　By whom?

SIR POLITIC　Sir, one, that though his place be obscure,
　Yet, he can sway, and they will hear him. He's
　A *commandadore*

83 *anticipate*   i.e. take advantage by putting the schemes into action before
       Sir Politic can.

86 *tinder-boxes*   boxes which carry fire-making materials.

91 **Arsenale**   the city's weapon store.

96 *suffered*   allowed.

98 *Sealed at some ... bigness*   Sir Politic ludicrously argues that all tinder-boxes
       should be licensed to be of a size which would prevent them being
       portable: this would prevent crimes of arson against the state.

101 *by present demonstration*   by an immediate test.

PEREGRINE   What, a common sergeant?
SIR POLITIC
   Sir, such as they are, put it in their mouths,
   What they should say, sometimes, as well as greater.   80
   I think I have my notes, to show you –

Searching his pockets

PEREGRINE   Good, sir.
SIR POLITIC
   But you shall swear unto me, on your gentry,
   Not to anticipate –
PEREGRINE   I, sir?
SIR POLITIC   Nor reveal
   A circumstance – My paper is not with me.
PEREGRINE
   O, but you can remember, sir.
SIR POLITIC   My first is,   85
   Concerning tinder-boxes. You must know,
   No family is here without its box.
   Now sir, it being so portable a thing,
   Put case, that you or I were ill affected
   Unto the state; sir, with it in our pockets,   90
   Might not I go into the *Arsenale*?
   Or you? come out again? and none the wiser?
PEREGRINE
   Except yourself, sir.
SIR POLITIC   Go to, then. I, therefore,
   Advèrtise to the state, how fit it were,
   That none but such as were known patriots,   95
   Sound lovers of their country, should be suffered
   T'enjoy them in their houses; and even those
   Sealed at some office, and at such a bigness,
   As might not lurk in pockets.
PEREGRINE   Admirable!
SIR POLITIC
   My next is, how t'enquire, and be resolved   100
   By present demonstration, whether a ship,

102 **Soria**   Syria.

105 *To lie out*   in quarantine until cleared for docking.

107 **Lazaretto**   islands off the coast used for quarantine.

110 *in onions*   Sir Politic's scheme revolves around the idea that onions absorb the plague virus and change colour with it. In proposing this, he is a grotesque parody of the mountebank with his fake cures, all of which are more likely to kill.

Newly arrivèd from *Soria*, or from
Any suspected part of all the Levant,
Be guilty of the plague; and, where they use
To lie out forty, fifty days, sometimes,   105
About the *Lazaretto* for their trial,
I'll save that charge and loss unto the merchant,
And, in an hour, clear the doubt.

PEREGRINE   Indeed, sir?

SIR POLITIC

Or – I will lose my labour.

PEREGRINE   My faith, that's much.

SIR POLITIC

Nay, sir, conceive me. 'Twill cost me, in onions,   110
Some thirty *livres* –

PEREGRINE   Which is one pound sterling.

SIR POLITIC

Beside my water-works; for this I do, sir.
First, I bring in your ship 'twixt two brick walls
(But those the state shall venture); on the one
I strain me a fair tarpaulin; and in that   115
I stick my onions, cut in halves; the other
Is full of loopholes, out at which I thrust
The noses of my bellows; and those bellows
I keep with waterworks in perpetual motion
(Which is the easiest matter of a hundred).   120
Now, sir, your onion, which doth naturally
Attract th'infection, and your bellows blowing
The air upon him, will show – instantly –
By his changed colour, if there be contagion;
Or else, remain as fair as at the first.   125
Now 'tis known, 'tis nothing.

PEREGRINE   You are right, sir.

SIR POLITIC

I would I had my note.

PEREGRINE   Faith, so would I;
But, you ha' done well, for once, sir.

128 *false* treacherous.

135–45 *Pray you ... politic notes!* Peregrine takes great pleasure in reading the trivial entries of a man who purports to be so important. He ends by concluding that they are 'politic' entries, apparently praising the knight yet making an ironic pun on his name and pretensions.

136–8 *A rat ... threshold* once again we see his superstition as he interprets an everyday occurrence as a portent and so takes evasive action.

141 **ragion del stato** affairs of the state. Like his attempt to use toothpicks, Sir Politic uses a smattering of Italian to make himself look cosmopolitan. The fact that this is in his own diary makes him look more ridiculous.

144 *I cheapened sprats* haggled over buying some sprats, already a cheap fish.

1 *loose* lascivious.

housed indoors with a prostitute.

SIR POLITIC   Were I false,
  Or would be made so, I could show you reasons
  How I could sell this state, now, to the Turk;   130
  Spite of their galleys, or their –

Examining his papers

PEREGRINE   Pray you, Sir Pol.
SIR POLITIC
  I have 'em not about me.
PEREGRINE   That I feared.
  They're there, sir?
SIR POLITIC   No, this is my diary,
  Wherein I note my actions of the day.
PEREGRINE
  Pray you, let's see, sir. What is here? '*Notandum,*   135
  A rat had gnawn my spur-leathers; notwithstanding,
  I put on new, and did go forth; but first
  I threw three beans over the threshold. *Item,*
  I went and bought two toothpicks, whereof one
  I burst immediately, in a discourse   140
  With a Dutch merchant 'bout *ragion del stato.*
  From him I went and paid a *moccenigo*
  For piecing my silk stockings; by the way
  I cheapened sprats; and at St Mark's, I urined.'
  Faith, these are politic notes!
SIR POLITIC   Sir, I do slip   145
  No action of my life, thus but I quote it.
PEREGRINE
  Believe me it is wise!
SIR POLITIC   Nay, sir, read forth.

Scene two

Enter at a distance LADY WOULD-BE, NANO, *two* WOMEN
LADY WOULD-BE
  Where should this loose knight be, trow? sure, he's housed.

2 **fast**   i.e. locked up and so not on the 'loose'. Nano is also playing with the saying 'fast and loose' and Lady Politic actually picks this up.

5 **I do not care ... him**   I don't want to stop him meeting her, I want to catch them at it. Lady Politic again shows a twisted morality here, particularly as she has just come from attempting to seduce Volpone. She is reminiscent of Corvino.

7–8 **That same's ... apparel**   Lady Would-be mistakes Peregrine for a prostitute in male clothes.

10 **demerit**   devalues it.

16 **Being your ... miss that**   Peregrine again manages to insult the knight without him realising.

20 **You mean ... today?**   Lady Would-be is referring to what she thinks is a disguise. She means that today is the first time the prostitute has appeared in this guise.

NANO
  Why, then he's fast.
LADY WOULD-BE   Ay, he plays both with me.
  I pray you, stay. This heat will do more harm
  To my complexion than his heart is worth.
  (I do not care to hinder, but to take him).   5
  How it comes off!

                                   Touching her make-up
1st WOMAN   My master's yonder.
LADY WOULD-BE   Where?
2nd WOMAN
  With a young gentleman.
LADY WOULD-BE   That same's the party!
  In man's apparel. Pray you, sir, jog my knight;
  I will be tender to his reputation,
  However he demerit.
SIR POLITIC   My lady!
PEREGRINE   Where?   10
SIR POLITIC
  'Tis she indeed, sir, you shall know her. She is,
  Were she not mine, a lady of that merit
  For fashion, and behaviour, and for beauty
  I durst compare –
PEREGRINE   It seems you are not jealous,
  That dare commend her.
SIR POLITIC   Nay, and for discourse –   15
PEREGRINE
  Being your wife, she cannot miss that.
SIR POLITIC (*As the groups meet*)   Madam,
  Here is a gentleman, pray you, use him fairly;
  He seems a youth, but he is –
LADY WOULD-BE   None?
SIR POLITIC   Yes, one,
  Has put his face as soon into the world –
LADY WOULD-BE
  You mean, as early? but today?

30 **Lord! ... oath** Peregrine means that even the knight's oaths show his background as he is unable to swear by his family name, but instead chooses an item of knightly apparel. Jonson is having a dig at the largesse of James I.

31 **I reach you not** I do not understand you.

35 **The Courtier** a guide book by Castiglione on courtly behaviour. By arguing in public, she is actually contravening its advice.

36 **rusticity** coarse behaviour.

42–3 **not warranted ... sex** not excused from being a crime against womanhood.

SIR POLITIC   How's this!   20
LADY WOULD-BE

Why, in this habit, sir, you apprehend me.
Well, Master Would-be, this doth not become you;
I had thought the odour, sir, of your good name
Had been more precious to you; that you would not
Have done this dire massàcre on your honour;   25
One of your gravity and rank besides!
But, knights, I see, care little for the oath
They make to ladies – chiefly, their own ladies.

SIR POLITIC

Now, by my spurs, the symbol of my knight-hood –

PEREGRINE (*Aside*)

Lord! how his brain is humbled for an oath.   30

SIR POLITIC

I reach you not.

LADY WOULD-BE   Right, sir, your polity

May bear it through thus. (*To* PEREGRINE) Sir, a word
    with you.
I would be loath to contest publicly
With any gentlewoman; or to seem
Froward or violent (as *The Courtier* says)   35
It comes too near rusticity in a lady,
Which I would shun by all means; and, however
I may deserve from Master Would-be, yet
T'have one fair gentlewoman thus be made
Th'unkind instrument to wrong another,   40
And one she knows not – ay, and to persèver –
In my poor judgement is not warranted
From being a solecism in our sex,
If not in manners.

PEREGRINE   How is this!

SIR POLITIC   Sweet Madam,

Come nearer to your aim.

LADY WOULD-BE   Marry, and will, sir.   45

Since you provoke me with your impudence

195

47–9 **light land-siren … storms**   she compares Peregrine to the mythical sirens
  who lured sailors to their deaths; to Sporus, the eunuch favoured by Nero
  so much that he disgraced himself by marrying him; and to a
  hermaphrodite. The latter insults arise out of the perceived disguise and
  add homosexuality to her accusations against Sir Politic.

  51 **Whitefriars**   a place favoured by prostitutes because, although it was in
  London, it was outside the City's jurisdiction so they could not be
  arrested.

  53 **forehead**   dignity.

  54 **St George**   patron saint of England. An ironic reference to one famous for
  saving damsels in distress.

  55 **fricatrice**   prostitute.

  58 **too liquid**   too clear. Sir Politic believes his wife's accusations.

  59 **your state face**   your serious face; self-righteous response.

  60 **carnival concupiscence**   'concupiscence' refers to strong sexual desire. The
  use of 'carnival' could either be an error, in that she could mean 'carnal', or
  be intended to contrast the riotous behaviour of the whore with the
  more moral behaviour of a society lady. Either way, the intended meaning,
  spat out in the alliterative phrase, is wanton whore.

  61 **liberty of conscience**   she suggests that prostitutes come to Venice – as
  religious outcasts do – for its atmosphere of tolerance. This one will have
  to flee the 'persecution' of the law Lady Would-be will bring down upon
  her.

  63 **disple**   whip.

  65 **'gainst you have occasion**   when you have the opportunity. Peregrine
  believes that her accusation was so ludicrous that it had to be a ruse. He
  now thinks that Sir Politic is a pimp for his wife.

And laughter of your light land-siren here,
Your Sporus, your hermaphrodite –

PEREGRINE   What's here?
Poetic fury, and historic storms!

SIR POLITIC
The gentleman, believe it, is of worth,   50
And of our nation.

LADY WOULD-BE   Ay, your Whitefriars nation!
Come, I blush for you, Master Would-be, ay!
And am ashamed you should ha' no more forehead
Than thus to be the patron, or St George,
To a lewd harlot, a base fricatrice,   55
A female devil in a male outside.

SIR POLITIC (*To* PEREGRINE)   Nay,
And you be such a one, I must bid adieu
To your delights! The case appears too liquid.

                                       Going

LADY WOULD-BE
Ay, you may carry 't clear, with your state-face!
But, for your carnival concupiscence,   60
Who here is fled for liberty of conscience,
From furious persecution of the marshal,
Her will I disple.

                        Exit SIR POLITIC

PEREGRINE   This is fine, i'faith!
And do you use this often? is this part
Of your wit's exercise, 'gainst you have occasion?   65
Madam –

LADY WOULD-BE Go to, sir.

         Snatching hold of PEREGRINE'S *clothing*

PEREGRINE   Do you hear me, lady?
Why if your knight have set you to beg shirts,
Or to invite me home, you might have done it
A nearer way, by far.

LADY WOULD-BE   This cannot work you
Out of my snare.

73 **to the queen-apple**   i.e. her nose is red, like this variety of apple.

2 **Right not my quest in this**   do not give me justice in this affair.
4 **callet**   prostitute.

Holding on still

PEREGRINE   Why? am I in it, then?   70
   Indeed, your husband told me you were fair,
   And so you are; only your nose inclines –
   That side that's next the sun – to the queen-apple.
LADY WOULD-BE
   This cannot be endured by any patience.

Scene three

Enter MOSCA
MOSCA
   What's the matter, madam?
LADY WOULD-BE   If the Senate
   Right not my quest in this, I will protest 'em,
   To all the world, no aristocracy.
MOSCA
   What is the injury, lady?
LADY WOULD-BE   Why, the callet
   You told me of, here I have ta'en disguised.   5
MOSCA
   Who? this? what means your ladyship? the creature
   I mentioned to you is apprehended now,
   Before the Senate; you shall see her –
LADY WOULD-BE   Where?
MOSCA
   I'll bring you to her. This young gentleman,
   I saw him land this morning at the port.   10
LADY WOULD-BE
   Is't possible! How has my judgment wandered!
   Sir, I must, blushing, say to you, I have erred,
   And plead your pardon.
PEREGRINE   What! more changes yet?

16 **please you to use me, sir**   having realised her mistake, she now confirms
     Peregrine's suspicions by offering herself to him. Like Corvino, one
     moment she is furiously jealous, the next minute wanton.

20 **Sir Politic Bawd!**   Sir Politic Pimp.

23 **salt-head**   experience. Peregrine thinks that he has been the victim of the
     kind of trick Sir Politic was ostensibly warning him against. He determines
     to have revenge.

1 **the carriage of the business**   Voltore is briefing the legacy-hunters on the
    parts they must play.

2 **constancy**   i.e. stick to your stories.

3–5 **Is the lie ... burden?**   does everyone understand the overall story? Is
     everyone certain of their parts?

6 **the advocate**   i.e. Voltore.

LADY WOULD-BE
  I hope you ha' not the malice to remember
  A gentlewoman's passion. If you stay   15
  In Venice here, please you to use me, sir –
MOSCA
  Will you go madam?
LADY WOULD-BE   Pray you, sir, use me. In faith,
  The more you see me, the more I shall conceive,
  You have forgot our quarrel.

Exeunt all except PEREGRINE
PEREGRINE   This is rare!
  Sir Politic Would-be? no, Sir Politic Bawd!   20
  To bring me thus acquainted with his wife!
  Well, wise Sir Pol, since you have practised thus
  Upon my freshmanship, I'll try your salt-head,
  What proof it is against a counter-plot.   *Exit*

Scene four

The Scrutineo
Enter VOLTORE, CORBACCIO, CORVINO, MOSCA
VOLTORE
  Well, now you know the carriage of the business,
  Your constancy is all that is required
  Unto the safety of it.
MOSCA   Is the lie
  Safely conveyed amongst us? is that sure?
  Knows every man his burden?
CORVINO   Yes.
MOSCA   Then shrink not.   5
CORVINO (*Aside to* MOSCA)
  But knows the advocate the truth?
MOSCA   O, sir,
  By no means. I devised a formal tale

8 **salved**   healed.

9–10 **his pleading ... co-heir**   even in this time of crisis Corvino thinks only of his inheritance. He fears that Voltore's skill as an advocate will win Volpone's favour.

10 **Co-halter!**   Mosca dismisses this derisively – Voltore can go hang himself!

12 **Croaker's**   i.e. Corbaccio.

14–19 **Sell him .... toil**   Mosca's audaciousness is almost admirable, as he reassures each in turn that the other is not a threat, even as they stand next to each other. To Corvino, Corbaccio is virtually mummified already; to Voltore, Corvino is a foolish cuckold; to Corbaccio, the others toil in vain to win the fortune. His aside, however, shows that his manoeuvring is difficult to keep up.

21 **Mercury**   messenger to the gods, he also watched over thieves.

22 **French Hercules**   god associated with eloquence as he persuaded Hippolyta, queen of the Amazons, to give him her girdle as one of his twelve labours. He is referred to as French as he is believed to have fathered the first of that race on his travels.

That salved your reputation. But be valiant, sir.

CORVINO

I fear no one but him; that this his pleading
Should make him stand for a co-heir –

MOSCA   Co-halter!   10
Hang him. We will but use his tongue, his noise,
As we do Croaker's here.

                               Pointing to CORBACCIO

CORVINO   Ay, what shall he do?

MOSCA

When we ha' done, you mean?

CORVINO   Yes.

MOSCA   Why, we'll think –
Sell him for mummia, he's half dust already.
(*To* VOLTORE) Do not you smile to see this buffalo,   15

                               (*Pointing to* CORVINO)

How he doth sport it with his head! – (*Aside*) I should,
If all were well and past.(*To* CORBACCIO) Sir, only you
Are he, that shall enjoy the crop of all,
And these not know for whom they toil.

CORBACCIO   Ay, peace.

MOSCA (*To* CORVINO)

But you shall eat it. (*Then to* VOLTORE *again*) Much!
        Worshipful sir,   20
Mercury sit upon your thund'ring tongue,
Or the French Hercules, and make your language
As conquering as his club, to beat along,
As with a tempest, flat, our adversaries;
But much more yours, sir.

VOLTORE   Here they come, ha' done.   25

MOSCA

I have another witness, if you need, sir,
I can produce.

VOLTORE   Who is it?

MOSCA   Sir, I have her.

203

5 ***The more ... father*** the most unnatural behaviour – that of Corbaccio.

6 ***More of the husband*** no, Corvino is worse.

8 ***the imposter*** i.e. Volpone.

9 ***And all after times!*** he will never be surpassed.

10 ***voluptuary*** a person addicted to sensual pleasures.

11 ***cited*** summoned.

16 ***pandar*** servant.

Scene five

Enter four AVOCATORI, BONARIO, CELIA, NOTARIO,
COMMANDADORI, *etc.*

1st AVOCATORE
  The like of this the Senate never heard of.
2nd AVOCATORE
  'Twill come most strange to them when we report it.
4th AVOCATORE
  The gentlewoman has been ever held
  Of unreprovèd name.
3rd AVOCATORE   So the young man.
4th AVOCATORE
  The more unnatural part that of his father.   5
2nd AVOCATORE
  More of the husband.
1st AVOCATORE   I do not know to give
  His act a name, it is so monstrous!
4th AVOCATORE
  But the imposter, he is a thing created
  T'exceed example!
1st AVOCATORE   And all after times!
2nd AVOCATORE
  I never heard a true voluptuary   10
  Described but him.
3rd AVOCATORE   Appear yet those were cited?
NOTARIO
  All but the old magnifico, Volpone.
1st AVOCATORE
  Why is not he here?
MOSCA   Please your fatherhoods,
  Here is his advocate. Himself's so weak,
  So feeble –
4th AVOCATORE What are you?
BONARIO   His parasite,   15
  His knave, his pandar. I beseech the court

25 *he may be heard in me*   I can plead on his behalf.

27 *crave it*   beg to be allowed to speak.

30 *strangely abusèd ears*   much deceived ears.

31 *frontless*   shameless.

37 *close*   secret.

40 *easy*   lenient. As part of the plot, Corvino is allowing himself to be described publicly not only as a cuckold, but one who forgave his wife to save his reputation.

41 *timeless*   ill-judged.

He may be forced to come, that your grave eyes
May bear strong witness of his strange impostures.

VOLTORE

Upon my faith and credit with your virtues,
He is not able to endure the air.   20

2nd AVOCATORE

Bring him, however.

3rd AVOCATORE   We will see him.

4th AVOCATORE   Fetch him.

Exeunt officers

VOLTORE

Your fatherhoods' fit pleasures be obeyed,
But sure, the sight will rather move your pities
Than indignation. May it please the court,
In the meantime, he may be heard in me.   25
I know this place most void of prejudice,
And therefore crave it, since we have no reason
To fear our truth should hurt our cause.

3rd AVOCATORE   Speak free.

VOLTORE

Then know, most honoured fathers, I must now
Discover to your strangely abusèd ears   30
The most prodigious and most frontless piece
Of solid impudence and treachery
That ever vicious nature yet brought forth
To shame the state of Venice. This lewd woman

(*Pointing to* CELIA)

(That wants no artificial looks or tears   35
To help the visor she has now put on)
Hath long been known a close adulteress
To that lascivious youth there; (*Pointing to* BONARIO) not
   suspected,
I say, but known; and taken in the act
With him; and by this man, the easy husband,   40

(*Pointing to* CORVINO)

Pardoned; whose timeless bounty makes him now

44–9 **not knowing ... such an act**   not knowing how to acknowledge a gift of such generosity, Celia and Bonario, steeped in sin, began to hate the memory of Corvino's virtuous forgiveness and plan how to get rid of it (i.e. to murder him).

64–5 **this settled ... know not**   was determined legally to disinherit him (but was betrayed in this intention by some unknown agency).

66 **parricide**   parent-killer. The charge will be developed in order to discredit Bonario. By striking Mosca, he has in some respects given credence to the picture of him as a violent man.

67–8 **by confederacy ... there**   this new elaborate story has Celia entering Volpone's house as part of Bonario's plan to murder his father. Her role would be to accuse Volpone of rape and so discredit him as an heir to Corbaccio's fortune.

70–1 **designed ... inheritance**   had chosen as his new heir.

Stand here, the most unhappy, innocent person
That ever man's own goodness made accused.
For these, not knowing how to owe a gift
Of that dear grace but with their shame – being placed   45
So above all powers of their gratitude –
Began to hate the benefit; and, in place
Of thanks, devise t'extirp the memory
Of such an act. Wherein, I pray your fatherhoods
To observe the malice, yea, the rage of creatures   50
Discovered in their evils; and what heart
Such take, even from their crimes. But that, anon,
Will more appear. This gentleman, the father,
                    (*Pointing to* CORBACCIO)
Hearing of this foul fact, with many others,
Which daily struck at his too tender ears,   55
And grieved in nothing more than that he could not
Preserve himself a parent (his son's ills
Growing to that strange flood) at last decreed
To disinherit him.
1st AVOCATORE   These be strange turns!
2nd AVOCATORE
The young man's fame was ever fair and honest.   60
VOLTORE
So much more full of danger is his vice,
That can beguile so, under shade of virtue.
But as I said, my honoured sires, his father
Having this settled purpose (by what means
To him betrayed, we know not) and this day   65
Appointed for the deed; that parricide
(I cannot style him better) by confederacy
Preparing this his paramour to be there,
Entered Volpone's house (who was the man
Your fatherhoods must understand, designed   70
For the inheritance), there sought his father.
But with what purpose sought he him, my lords?
I tremble to pronounce it, that a son

79 **Mischief . . . . it begins** mischief is capable of any gross deed. Considering the actions of the defendants, it is heavily ironic that they should employ such a moral.

85 **The stale to . . . practice** the bait in his false plotting.

87–8 **note but . . . remarkable** to listen carefully to my conclusions, which are truly enlightening.

91 **laying infamy upon this man** besmirching the good name of Corvino.

95 **mercenary** hired.

97 **sols** small coins.

99 **scope** freedom to speak. Voltore is happy to let Bonario rave, as his seemingly wild accusations are clearly creating a bad impression with the judges.

Unto a father, and to such a father,
Should have so foul, felonious intent.   75
It was, to murder him! When, being prevented
By his more happy absence, what then did he?
Not check his wicked thoughts; no, now new deeds –
Mischief doth ever end where it begins –
An act of horror, fathers! He dragged forth   80
The agèd gentleman, that had there lain bed-rid
Three years and more, out off his innocent couch,
Naked, upon the floor; there left him; wounded
His servant in the face; and, with this strumpet,
The stale to his forged practice, who was glad   85
To be so active (I shall here desire
Your fatherhoods to note but my collections
As most remarkable) thought at once to stop
His father's ends, discredit his free choice
In the old gentleman, redeem themselves   90
By laying infamy upon this man,

                    (*Pointing to* CORVINO)

To whom, with blushing, they should owe their lives.

1st AVOCATORE

What proofs have you of this?

BONARIO   Most honoured fathers,

  I humbly crave there be no credit given

  To this man's mercenary tongue.

2nd AVOCATORE   Forbear.   95

BONARIO

  His soul moves in his fee.

3rd AVOCATORE   O, sir.

BONARIO   This fellow,

  For six sols more, would plead against his Maker.

1st AVOCATORE

  You do forget yourself.

VOLTORE   Nay, nay, grave fathers,

  Let him have scope. Can any man imagine

102   *a creature*   a human being because, as such, she cannot take her own life.

106–7   *my heart ... in him*   my heart hates his existence. I disclaim any part of me in him i.e. I refuse to acknowledge him as my son. Ironically, Corbaccio is acting exactly as Mosca first said he would when he baited Bonario in Act 3, scene 2.

110   *Have they made you to this!*   even now, Bonario cannot believe his father capable of such acts.

114   *resist the authority of a father*   Bonario's filial loyalty makes Corbaccio's act seem all the more unnatural. The response does show, however, the weakness of virtue in the face of sin.

That he will spare his accuser, that would not   100
Have spared his parent?

1st AVOCATORE   Well, produce your proofs.

CELIA

I would I could forget I were a creature.

VOLTORE

Signior Corbaccio!

4th AVOCATORE   What is he?

VOLTORE   The father.

2nd AVOCATORE

Has he had an oath?

NOTARIO   Yes.

CORBACCIO   What must I do now?

NOTARIO

Your testimony's craved.

CORBACCIO   Speak to the knave?   105
I'll ha' my mouth first stopped with earth; my heart
Abhors his knowledge. I disclaim in him.

1st AVOCATORE

But for what cause?

CORBACCIO   The mere portent of nature.
He is an utter stranger to my loins.

BONARIO

Have they made you to this!

CORBACCIO   I will not hear thee,   110
Monster of men, swine, goat, wolf, parricide,
Speak not, thou viper.

BONARIO   Sir, I will sit down,
And rather wish my innocence should suffer,
Than I resist the authority of a father.

VOLTORE

Signior Corvino!

2nd AVOCATORE   This is strange!

1st AVOCATORE   Who's this?   115

NOTARIO

The husband.

118 **Of most hot ... partridge** of such a lustful spirit that she outdoes the
partridge (which was renowned for this).

119 **Neighs like a jennet** a Spanish mare. Celia is once more pictured as
inappropriate animals. The contrast again says more about the speaker
than her.

123–4 **glued ... gallant** Corvino uses the wood image to refer to Bonario's build.
His description of their sexual encounters is intended by him to arouse
the judges' disgust; it has exactly the same effect on the audience but he is
the target of our loathing, particularly as he is describing his wife.

125 **The letters ... horn** to convince the judges, he proclaims himself a cuckold
by saying that he sports the signatory letter 'V' and the traditional horns.
He is blind to the infamy he is heaping upon himself, which will be
doubled when the truth is revealed.

127 **There is no shame ... is there?** his question to Mosca shows just how blind
he is.

4th AVOCATORE Is he sworn?

NOTARIO   He is.

3rd AVOCATORE   Speak then.

CORVINO

This woman, please your fatherhoods, is a whore
Of most hot exercise, more than a partridge,
Upon recòrd –

1st AVOCATORE   No more.

CORVINO   Neighs like a jennet.

NOTARIO

Preserve the honour of the court.

CORVINO   I shall,   120
And modesty of your most reverend ears.
And yet I hope that I may say, these eyes
Have seen her glued unto that piece of cedar,
                        (*Pointing to* BONARIO)
That fine well-timbered gallant; and that here
                        (*Touching his forehead*)
The letters may be read, thorough the horn,   125
That make the story perfect.

MOSCA (*Aside to* CORVINO)   Excellent! sir.

CORVINO (*To* MOSCA)

There is no shame in this now, is there?

MOSCA   None.

CORVINO

Or if I said, I hoped that she were onward
To her damnation, if there be a hell
Greater than whore, and woman – a good Catholic   130
May make the doubt.

3rd AVOCATORE   His grief hath made him frantic.

1st AVOCATORE

Remove him hence.

2nd AVOCATORE   Look to the woman.

                            She swoons

CORVINO   Rare!
Prettily feigned! again!

215

139 **most laid**   carefully plotted.

145 **Unsatisfied**   insatiable. Corvino cannot resist adding more but, in doing so, brings more ridicule upon himself: the suggestion is that he was incapable of satisfying his wife.

4th AVOCATORE   Stand from about her.

1st AVOCATORE

  Give her the air.

3rd AVOCATORE (*To* MOSCA) What can you say?

MOSCA   My wound,

  May't please your wisdoms, speaks for me, received   135

  In aid of my good patron, when he missed

                                  (*Pointing to* BONARIO)

  His sought-for father, when that well-taught dame

  Had her cue given to cry out a rape.

BONARIO

  O, most laid impudence! Fathers –

3rd AVOCATORE   Sir, be silent,

  You had your hearing free, so must they theirs.   140

2nd AVOCATORE

  I do begin to doubt th'imposture here.

4th AVOCATORE

  This woman has too many moods.

VOLTORE   Grave fathers,

  She is a creature of a most professed

  And prostituted lewdness.

CORVINO   Most impetuous!

  Unsatisfied, grave fathers!

VOLTORE   May her feignings   145

  Not take your wisdoms; but this day, she baited

  A stranger, a grave knight, with her loose eyes,

  And more lascivious kisses. This man saw 'em

  Together on the water, in a gondola.

MOSCA

  Here is the lady herself, that saw 'em too,   150

  Without; who then had in the open streets

  Pursued them, but for saving her knight's honour.

1st AVOCATORE

  Produce that lady.

2nd AVOCATORE   Let her come.

                                    Exit MOSCA

                                        217

2 **chameleon**   an ironic description, as Celia is one of the few characters who cannot change their appearance/nature in the play. The accuser is in the process of doing this, taking on the guise of the wronged wife in order to ensure personal gain.

3 **Vie tears with the hyena!**   the hyena was a symbol of treachery because it was believed it simulated a human cry to lure its victims.

7 **exorbitant**   outrageous in my language.

13 **pertinacy**   she could mean impertinence: cheek, or pertinacity: over-insistence.

4th AVOCATORE   These things,
   They strike with wonder!
3rd AVOCATORE   I am turned a stone!

Scene six

(*Enter* MOSCA *with* LADY WOULD-BE)
MOSCA
   Be resolute, madam.
LADY WOULD-BE   Ay, this same is she.

                            (*Pointing to* CELIA)
   Out, thou chameleon harlot! Now thine eyes
   Vie tears with the hyena! Dar'st thou look
   Upon my wrongèd face? I cry your pardons.
   I fear, I have (forgettingly) transgressed   5
   Against the dignity of the court –
2nd AVOCATORE   No, madam.
LADY WOULD-BE
   And been exorbitant –
4th AVOCATORE   You have not, lady.
1st AVOCATORE
   These proofs are strong.
LADY WOULD-BE   Surely, I had no purpose
   To scandalize your honours, or my sex's.
3rd AVOCATORE
   We do believe it.
LADY WOULD-BE   Surely, you may believe it.   10
2nd AVOCATORE
   Madam, we do.
LADY WOULD-BE   Indeed, you may; my breeding
   Is not so coarse –
4th AVOCATORE   We know it.
LADY WOULD-BE   To offend
   With pertinacy –
3rd AVOCATORE   Lady.

15 **Let her o'ercome** let her have the last word. The calling of Lady Would-be by Mosca is a master-stroke as, given her garrulousness, it is guaranteed to get the judges to finish the case quickly, if only to shut her up.

19 **Where multitude ... overcomes** Bonario picks up on the judge's dismissal of conscience and heaven as forces in the court. He is accusing the *avocatori* of being blind to virtue, listening instead only to those who are the most skilled in language.

20 **wax** become.

25 **The grand voluptuary!** Voltore pours scorn on the earlier description, given Volpone's decrepit appearance.

27 **Covet a concubine** look lustfully for a prostitute.

31–2 **goads ... strappado** Voltore has lured Bonario into a trap by getting him to say that he would like proof of Volpone's illness. This is now interpreted by the lawyer as wanting the sick man to be interrogated with the use of pointed sticks ('goads'), branding irons or the '*strappado*', a crude form of the rack, in which a person was suspended by his arms, which had been tied behind his back.

LADY WOULD-BE   Such a presence.
  No, surely.
1st AVOCATORE We well think it.
LADY WOULD-BE   You may think it.
1st AVOCATORE
  Let her o'ercome. (*To* BONARIO) What witnesses have you,   15
  To make good your report?
BONARIO   Our consciences.
CELIA
  And heaven, that never fails the innocent.
4th AVOCATORE
  These are no testimonies.
BONARIO   Not in your courts,
  Where multitude and clamour overcomes.
1st AVOCATORE
  Nay, then you do wax insolent.
VOLTORE   Here, here,   20
                    (VOLPONE *is brought in, as impotent*)
  The testimony comes that will convince
  And put to utter dumbness their bold tongues
  See here, grave fathers, here's the ravisher,
  The rider on men's wives, the great impostor,
  The grand voluptuary! Do you not think   25
  These limbs should affect venery? or these eyes
  Covet a concubine? Pray you, mark these hands –
  Are they not fit to stroke a lady's breasts?
  Perhaps he doth dissemble?
BONARIO   So he does.
VOLTORE
  Would you ha' him tortured?
BONARIO   I would have him proved.   30
VOLTORE
  Best try him then with goads, or burning irons;
  Put him to the *strappado;* I have heard
  The rack hath cured the gout, faith, give it him,
  And help him of a malady – be courteous.

42 **traduce**   slander. Voltore argues that if such great injustices are left unpunished, then no one is safe from slander. He frightens the judges by making them think that they will be creating a precedent for disorder.

51–2 **That vicious … abounds**   that vicious people, when they have the taste for doing terrible deeds, are consistent in their actions. The irony is that his conclusion is more fitting to the new accusers than to the accused couple.

55 **prodigies**   monsters.

I'll undertake, before these honoured fathers,   35
He shall have yet as many left diseases
As she has known adulterers, or thou strumpets.
O, my most equal hearers, if these deeds,
Acts of this bold and most exorbitant strain,
May pass with sufferance, what one citizen   40
But owes the forfeit of his life, yea fame,
To him that dares traduce him? Which of you
Are safe, my honoured fathers? I would ask
(With leave of your grave fatherhoods) if their plot
Have any face, or colour, like to truth?   45
Or if, unto the dullest nostril here,
It smell not rank and most abhorrèd slander?
I crave your care of this good gentleman,
Whose life is much endangered by their fable;
And, as for them, I will conclude with this: 50
That vicious persons when they are hot and fleshed
In impious acts, their constancy abounds;
Damned deeds are done with greatest confidence.

1st AVOCATORE

    Take 'em to custody, and sever them.

                       CELIA *and* BONARIO *are taken out*

2nd AVOCATORE

    'Tis pity two such prodigies should live.   55

1st AVOCATORE

    Let the old gentleman be returned with care;
    I'm sorry our credulity wronged him.

                          VOLPONE *is carried off*

4th AVOCATORE

    These are two creatures!

3rd AVOCATORE   I have an earthquake in me!

2nd AVOCATORE

    Their shame, even in their cradles, fled their faces.

4th AVOCATORE [*To* VOLTORE]

    You've done a worthy service to the state, sir,   60
    In their discovery.

71 **the other** i.e. that you tried to prostitute your wife.

1st AVOCATORE   You shall hear ere night
  What punishment the court decrees upon 'em
VOLTORE
  We thank your fatherhoods.

> (*Exeunt* AVOCATORI, NOTARIO, OFFICER)
> How like you it?

MOSCA   Rare.
  I'd ha' your tongue, sir, tipped with gold for this;
  I'd ha' you be the heir to the whole city;   65
  The earth I'd have want men, ere you want living.
  They're bound to erect your statue in St Mark's.
  Signior Corvino, I would have you go
  And show yourself, that you have conquered.
CORVINO   Yes.
MOSCA
  It was much better that you should profess   70
  Yourself a cuckold thus, than that the other
  Should have been proved.
CORVINO   Nay, I considered that;
  Now, it is her fault –
MOSCA   Then, it had been yours.
CORVINO
  True. I do doubt this advocate still.
MOSCA   I'faith,
  You need not; I dare ease you of that care.   75
CORVINO
  I trust thee, Mosca.
MOSCA   As your own soul, sir.

> *Exit* CORVINO
CORBACCIO   Mosca!
MOSCA
  Now for your business, sir.
CORBACCIO   How? ha' you business?
MOSCA
  Yes, yours, sir.

225

78 **Rest you ... eyes**   i.e. you do not have to keep an eye open looking for treachery as I will take care of you.

85 **I must tender it**   Mosca must keep them apart as much as possible. The last thing he wants is for Corbaccio to be proclaiming himself Volpone's heir to Voltore.

   Two chequeens   two gold coins. Now the trial is over, and they are safe, all unity between the legacy-hunters falls apart and they return to their avaricious ways. They have briefly been a pack; now they are lone scavengers once more.

91 **Worthy this age?**   that he could become so unnatural now that he is getting old.

CORBACCIO	O, none else?
MOSCA	None else, not I.
CORBACCIO	

Be careful then.

MOSCA	Rest you, with both your eyes, sir.
CORBACCIO	

Dispatch it.

MOSCA	Instantly.
CORBACCIO	And look that all

Whatever be put in: jewels, plate, moneys,
Household stuff, bedding, curtains.

MOSCA   Curtain-rings, sir –
Only, the advocate's fee must be deducted.

CORBACCIO

I'll pay him now – you'll be too prodigal.

MOSCA

Sir, I must tender it.

CORBACCIO   Two chequeens is well?

MOSCA

No, six, sir.

CORBACCIO   'Tis too much.

MOSCA   He talked a great while,
You must consider that, sir.

CORBACCIO   Well, there's three –

MOSCA

I'll give it him.

CORBACCIO   Do so, and there's for thee.

                                   Exit CORBACCIO

MOSCA

Bountiful bones! What horrid strange offence
Did he commit 'gainst nature in his youth,
Worthy this age? you see, sir, (*To* VOLTORE) how I work
Unto your ends; take you no notice.

VOLTORE   No,
I'll leave you.

MOSCA   All is yours (*Exit* VOLTORE) – the devil
and all,

80

85

90

227

    Good advocate. – (*To* LADY WOULD-BE) Madam, I'll
      bring you home.
LADY WOULD-BE
    No, I'll go see your patron.
MOSCA   That you shall not.   95
    I'll tell you why: my purpose is to urge
    My patron to reform his will; and, for
    The zeal you've shown today, whereas before
    You were but third or fourth, you shall be now
    Put in the first; which would appear as begged   100
    If you were present. Therefore –
LADY WOULD-BE   You shall sway me.

                                    Exeunt

2 **Till this fled moment**   until just a moment ago.

4 **But in your public – Cavè**   Volpone realises that he is virtually untouchable in disguise when in his own house but that, like his namesake, he is most in danger when out of his lair. However, he is unable to contain his natural exuberance for long and will soon risk all once more for the thrill of pitting his own ingenuity against chance, ignoring the warning he has given himself.

7 **dead palsy**   fatal paralysis.

14 **device**   plot.

16 **Would make me up again**   make me feel myself again.

17 **This heat ... this time**   the wine brings with it the heat of life; I have absorbed it into my bloodstream already.

2–3 **and wrought ... way?**   rescued from error back on to the righteous path? Mosca is gloating on his triumph, once more mocking those who put their faith in religion as he feels they have conclusively defeated virtue.

Act Five

Scene one

VOLPONE'S *House*
Enter VOLPONE
VOLPONE

Well, I am here; and all this brunt is past.
I ne'er was in dislike with my disguise
Till this fled moment; here, 'twas good, in private,
But in your public – *Cavè*, whilst I breathe.
'Fore God, my left leg 'gan to have the cramp,   5
And I apprehended, straight, some power had struck me
With a dead palsy. Well, I must be merry,
And shake it off. A many of these fears
Would put me into some villainous disease,
Should they come thick upon me – I'll prevent 'em.   10
Give me a bowl of lusty wine, to fright
This humour from my heart. (*He drinks*) Hum, hum,
    hum!
'Tis almost gone, already – I shall conquer.
Any device, now, of rare, ingenious knavery,
That would possess me with a violent laughter,   15
Would make me up again! (*Drinks again*) So, so, so, so.
This heat is life; 'tis blood by this time. Mosça!

Scene two

Enter MOSCA
MOSCA

How now, sir? does the day look clear again?
Are we recovered? and wrought out of error
Into our way? to see our path before us?
Is our trade free once more?

5 ***carried learnedly***   brought off expertly.

6 ***Good wits ... extremities***   this could explain why they put themselves at risk
   so much – the need constantly to show their superior intelligence.

9 ***You are not ... methinks***   I think you are not enraptured with our triumph.

14 ***Thou'st played thy prize***   you have played your masterpiece. Mosca
   encourages praise by seeming to deny this and then elaborating on his
   triumph.

VOLPONE   Exquisite Mosca!
MOSCA
  Was it not carried learnedly?
VOLPONE   And stoutly.   5
  Good wits are greatest in extremities.
MOSCA
  It were a folly beyond thought to trust
  Any grand act unto a cowardly spirit.
  You are not taken with it enough, methinks?
VOLPONE
  O, more than if I had enjoyed the wench;   10
  The pleasure of all womankind's not like it.
MOSCA
  Why, now you speak, sir. We must here be fixed;
  Here we must rest; this is our masterpiece;
  We cannot think to go beyond this.
VOLPONE   True,
  Thou'st played thy prize, my precious Mosca.
MOSCA   Nay, sir,   15
  To gull the court –
VOLPONE   And quite divert the torrent
  Upon the innocent.
MOSCA   Yes, and to make
  So rare a music out of discords –
VOLPONE   Right.
  That yet to me's the strangest! how thou'st borne it!
  That these, being so divided 'mongst themselves,   20
  Should not scent somewhat, or in me or thee,
  Or doubt their own side.
MOSCA   True, they will not see't.
  Too much light blinds 'em, I think. Each of 'em
  Is so possessed, and stuffed with his own hopes,
  That anything unto the contrary,   25
  Never so true, or never so apparent,
  Never so palpable, they will resist it –

28 *Like a temptation ... devil*   Volpone is right in that much of what Mosca does is reminiscent of a stage devil, tempting men to pander to the weaknesses which will destroy them.

31 *any glebe*   soil.

40 *A little in a mist*   temporarily disorientated.

47 *to be cozened*   to be cheated.

50 *aggravate*   expand upon his arguments.

51 *vehement figures*   stirring metaphors.

52 *shift a shirt*   change his shirt, because the vigour of his performance was making him sweat so.

53 *no hope of gain*   Mosca is of course being ironic. His overall description of Voltore is intended to draw his master into pitting his wits against him again.

VOLPONE

Like a temptation of the devil.

MOSCA   Right, sir.

Merchants may talk of trade, and your great signiors

Of land that yields well; but if Italy   30

Have any glebe more fruitful than these fellows,

I am deceived. Did not your advocate rare?

VOLPONE

O – 'My most honoured fathers, my grave fathers,

Under correction of your fatherhoods,

What face of truth is here? If these strange deeds   35

May pass, most honoured fathers' – I had much ado

To forbear laughing.

MOSCA   'T seemed to me, you sweat, sir.

VOLPONE

In troth, I did a little.

MOSCA   But confess, sir.

Were you not daunted?

VOLPONE   In good faith, I was

A little in a mist; but not dejected –   40

Never but still myself.

MOSCA   I think it, sir.

Now, so truth help me, I must needs say this, sir,

And, out of conscience, for your advocate:

He's taken pains, in faith, sir, and deserved,

(In my poor judgment, I speak it, under favour,   45

Not to contrary you, sir) very richly –

Well – to be cozened.

VOLPONE   Troth, and I think so too,

By that I heard him, in the latter end.

MOSCA

O, but before, sir; had you heard him first

Draw it to certain heads, then aggravate,   50

Then use his vehement figures – I looked still

When he would shift a shirt; and, doing this

Out of pure love, no hope of gain –

66 **she-wolf** Lady Would-be.

68 **And then ... mouths?** Mosca relishes the moment the suitors will find Volpone alive. He has not yet realised the magnitude of the plan.

72 **blanks** i.e. blank spaces for the heir's name. Volpone intends to spite them by naming his parasite as his heir. He does not realise the change in Mosca, nor does he think the plot through: if his parasite is legally his heir and he is recognised as dead, what recourse can he have if Mosca decides to act against him? In effect, the plan puts him at the mercy of a man whose whole life has centred around acquiring wealth by feeding off him.

VOLPONE   'Tis right.
I cannot answer him, Mosca, as I would,
Not yet; but, for thy sake, at thy entreaty,   55
I will begin, even now, to vex 'em all,
This very instant.
MOSCA   Good, sir.
VOLPONE   Call the dwarf
And eunuch forth.
MOSCA   Castrone, Nano!

Enter CASTRONE *and* NANO
NANO   Here.
VOLPONE
Shall we have a jig now?
MOSCA   What you please, sir.
VOLPONE   Go,
Straight, give out about the streets, you two,   60
That I am dead; do it with constancy,
Sadly, do you hear? Impute it to the grief
Of this late slander.

Exeunt CASTRONE *and* NANO
MOSCA   What do you mean, sir?
VOLPONE   O,
I shall have instantly my vulture, crow,
Raven, come flying hither on the news,   65
To peck for carrion, my she-wolf and all,
Greedy, and full of expectation –
MOSCA
And then to have it ravished from their
     mouths?
VOLPONE
'Tis true, I will ha' thee put on a gown
And take upon thee as thou wert mine heir;   70
Show 'em a will – open that chest, and reach
Forth one of those that has the blanks. I'll straight
Put in thy name.
MOSCA   It will be rare, sir.

74 **_gape_** the image is once more an echo of the fable of the fox and the crow.

77 **_corrupted_** decomposing. The description is ironic if we take the adjective literally – it describes Volpone's moral state.

88 **_stark dull_** in contrast to his sharpness at the trial.

90 **clarissimo** grandee or nobleman (Corbaccio).

91 **_crump you_** curl up.

93 **_a rope and a dagger_** traditional weapons for suicide.

VOLPONE   Ay,
When they e'en gape, and find themselves deluded –
MOSCA
Yes.
VOLPONE And thou use them scurvily. Dispatch,   75
Get on thy gown.
MOSCA   But, what, sir, if they ask
After the body?
VOLPONE   Say it was corrupted.
MOSCA
I'll say it stunk, sir; and was fain t'have it
Coffined up instantly, and sent away.
VOLPONE
Anything, what thou wilt. Hold, here's my will.   80
Get thee a cap, a count-book, pen and ink,
Papers afore thee; sit as thou wert taking
An inventory of parcels. I'll get up
Behind the curtain on a stool, and hearken;
Sometime, peep over; see how they do look;   85
With what degrees their blood doth leave their faces!
O, 'twill afford me a rare meal of laughter.
MOSCA
Your advocate will turn stark dull upon it.
VOLPONE
It will take off his oratory's edge.
MOSCA
But your *clarissimo*, old round-back, he   90
Will crump you, like a hog-louse, with the touch.
VOLPONE
And what Corvino?
MOSCA   O, sir, look for him
Tomorrow morning, with a rope and a dagger,
To visit all the streets; he must run mad.
My lady too, that came into the court   95
To bear false witness for your worship –
VOLPONE   Yes,

98 **And sweat** Mosca again reminds Volpone of his weakness and again is not admonished. It is almost as if he is trying to see how far he can go.

102 **strange poetical girdle** the girdle of Venus, reputed to be capable of beautifying even the most hideous.

102–4 **Jove ... Acrisius' guards** Mosca refers to the myth by which Acrisius locked his daughter in a tower to prevent her from having children as he had been warned that her son would kill him. Jove, tempted by the challenge, passed by the guards in a shower of gold and ravished her. The speech seems nonsensical until one realises that Mosca must be imitating Lady Would-be.

111 **artificer** craftsman e.g. torture them expertly.

And kissed me 'fore the fathers, when my face
Flowed all with oils.
MOSCA   And sweat, sir. Why, your gold
Is such another med'cine, it dries up
All those offensive savours! It transforms   100
The most deformèd, and restores 'em lovely,
As 'twere the strange poetical girdle. Jove
Could not invent t'himself a shroud more subtle
To pass Acrisius' guards. It is the thing
Makes all the world her grace, her youth, her beauty.   105
VOLPONE
I think she loves me.
MOSCA   Who? the lady, sir?
She's jealous of you.
VOLPONE   Dost thou say so?

Knocking without

MOSCA   Hark,
There's some already.
VOLPONE   Look.
MOSCA   It is the vulture;
He has the quickest scent.
VOLPONE   I'll to my place,

(Concealing himself)

Thou, to thy posture.
MOSCA   I am set.
VOLPONE   But Mosca,   110
Play the artificer now, torture 'em rarely.

Scene three

Enter VOLTORE
VOLTORE
How now, my Mosca?
MOSCA   Turkey carpets, nine –

3 **tissue**   a rich cloth interwoven with gold.

11 **Is his thread spun?**   a classical allusion meaning, 'Is he dead?' So much for
Volpone's feeling she was in love with him.

14 **diaper ... damask**   both were expensive types of linen.

VOLTORE

  Taking an inventory? that is well.

MOSCA

  Two suits of bedding, tissue –

VOLTORE   Where's the will?

  Let me read that the while.

Enter CORBACCIO *carried in a chair*

CORBACCIO   So, set me down,

  And get you home.

                              Exeunt BEARERS

VOLTORE   Is he come, now, to trouble us?   5

MOSCA Of cloth of gold, two more –

CORBACCIO   Is it done, Mosca?

MOSCA

  Of several velvets, eight –

VOLTORE   I like his care.

CORBACCIO

  Dost thou not hear?

Enter CORVINO

CORVINO   Ha! is the hour come, Mosca?

             VOLPONE *peeps from behind a traverse*

VOLPONE (*Aside*)

  Ay, now they muster.

CORVINO   What does the advocate here?

  Or this Corbaccio?

CORBACCIO   What do these here?

Enter LADY WOULD-BE

LADY WOULD-BE   Mosca!   10

  Is his thread spun?

MOSCA   Eight chests of linen –

VOLPONE (*Aside*)   O,

  My fine dame Would-be, too!

CORVINO   Mosca, the will,

  That I may show it these, and rid 'em hence.

MOSCA

  Six chests of diaper, four of damask – There.

                         Gives them the will

20 **_hangings_**   wall hangings, for a bedroom.

21 **_Ay, i'their garters_**   Volpone, enjoying the spectacle, picks up on the word and laughs at the way the suitors are figuratively choking with indignation. He rightly says their dreams are dying ('at the gasp').

25 **_Old glazen-eyes_**   Corbaccio wears glasses so it takes him longer to get through the will.

26–7 **_All these … the man_**   the comedy is heightened here as Corbaccio watches the others' reaction and assumes he is the heir.

30 **_I am very busy_**   Mosca plays his part to the full, ignoring their reaction and dismissing them contemptuously in order to provoke their rage further.

CORBACCIO

   Is that the will?

MOSCA   Down-beds; and bolsters –

VOLPONE (*Aside*)   Rare!   15

   Be busy still. Now they begin to flutter –

   They never think of me. Look, see, see, see!

   How their swift eyes run over the long deed

   Unto the name, and to the legacies,

   What is bequeathed them there –

MOSCA   Ten suits of hangings   20

VOLPONE (*Aside*)

   Ay, i'their garters, Mosca. Now their hopes

   Are at the gasp.

VOLTORE   Mosca the heir!

CORBACCIO   What's that?

VOLPONE (*Aside*)

  My advocate is dumb. Look to my merchant –

  He has heard of some strange storm, a ship is lost;

  He faints. My lady will swoon. Old glazen-eyes,   25

  He hath not reached his despair, yet.

CORBACCIO   All these

   Are out of hope; I am sure the man.

CORVINO   But, Mosca –

MOSCA

   Two cabinets –

CORVINO   Is this in earnest?

MOSCA   One

   Of ebony –

CORVINO   Or do you but delude me?

MOSCA

   The other, mother of pearl – I am very busy.   30

   Good faith, it is a fortune thrown upon me –

   Item, one salt of agate – not my seeking.

36   ***Is this my large hope's issue?***   is this my recompense for such a huge outlay?

38   ***my house***   the possessive adjective is guaranteed to infuriate her.

40–5   ***Remember ... melancholic***   in response to her threatening demeanour, Mosca reminds her that she has promised sexual favours in exchange for him praising her to Volpone. The suggestion has been made that this happens at the end of Act 4 yet there is nothing in the text to justify this. It would seem a strange omission by Johnson yet we must accept that the episode has happened as Lady Would-be leaves when Mosca blackmails her with the thought of being revealed as willing to do what 'your best madams' do for gain.

48   ***been th'example***   Mosca now turns on Corvino, telling him contemptuously that he should have led the way out of the house.

50–3   ***an ass? ... good terms***   as he plays his part, one can sense the relish with which Mosca tells the suitors exactly what he thinks of them. He dismisses each by opening their eyes to exactly what they have done, here telling Corvino that he has acted as a fool; has been willing to tolerate his wife's adultery, even to the point of encouraging it; and has professed himself a cuckold in public.

LADY WOULD-BE

  Do you hear, sir?

MOSCA   A perfumed box – pray you forbear,

  You see I am troubled – made of an onyx –

LADY WOULD-BE   How!

MOSCA

  Tomorrow, or next day, I shall be at leisure   35

  To talk with you all.

CORVINO   Is this my large hope's issue?

LADY WOULD-BE

  Sir, I must have a fairer answer.

MOSCA   Madam!

  Marry, and shall: pray you, fairly quit my house.

  Nay, raise no tempest with your looks; but hark you:

  Remember what your ladyship offered me   40

  To put you in an heir; go to, think on't.

  And what you said e'en your best madams did

  For maintenance, and why not you? Enough.

  Go home, and use the poor Sir Pol, your knight, well,

  For fear I tell some riddles. Go, be melancholic.   45

                           Exit LADY WOULD-BE

VOLPONE (*Aside*)

  O, my fine devil!

CORVINO   Mosca, pray you a word.

MOSCA

  Lord! will not you take your dispatch hence yet?

  Methinks, of all, you should have been th'example.

  Why should you stay here? with what thought? what

    promise?

  Hear you, do not you know, I know you an ass?   50

  And that you would, most fain, have been a wittol,

  If fortune would have let you? that you are

  A declared cuckold, on good terms? This pearl,

  You'll say, was yours? Right. This diamond?

  I'll not deny't, but thank you. Much here else?   55

  It may be so. Why, think that these good works

57 **I'll not betray you**   Mosca's seeming loyalty is nothing more than a vicious put-down. Corvino is an extraordinary cuckold because he has accepted the title without deserving it. However, Mosca will not betray this foolishness because to do so would be to reveal his grosser crime. Hence the pledge is actually blackmail.

61 **Rare ... becomes him**   the aside is ironic. Volpone is expressing glee at Mosca's contempt without realising he is now as powerless as the suitors. Mosca's villainy becomes him because it is not a charade, as he will soon realise.

63 **Mosca, the heir?**   Corbaccio at last realises what the others are upset about.

68 **the three legs**   Corbaccio's infirmity is once more ridiculed, this time because he walks with a stick.

69–70 **snuffed ... nose**   the porcine image conveys Mosca's distaste. He goes on to list the old man's crimes, once again showing that he is open to blackmail.

74 **and die, and stink**   once again Corbaccio is dealt with most harshly because his infirmity makes him unable to strike out. 'Stink' is repeated, forcing home the message that it is his corruption which will smell.

78 **constancy**   Voltore misjudges Mosca's actions, thinking they are a sign that he will give him all when the others have gone.

May help to hide your bad – I'll not betray you.
Although you be but extraordinary,
And have it only in title, it sufficeth.
Go home, be melancholic too, or mad. 60

Exit CORVINO

VOLPONE (*Aside*)
Rare, Mosca! how his villainy becomes him!
VOLTORE
Certain, he doth delude all these for me.
CORBACCIO
Mosca, the heir?
VOLPONE (*Aside*) O, his four eyes have found it!
CORBACCIO
I'm cozened, cheated, by a parasite slave;
Harlot, thou'st gulled me.
MOSCA Yes, sir. Stop your mouth, 65
Or I shall draw the only tooth, is left.
Are not you he, that filthy covetous wretch
With the three legs, that here, in hope of prey,
Have, any time this three year, snuffed about
With your most grov'ling nose; and would have hired 70
Me to the pois'ning of my patron? Sir?
Are not you he that have, today, in court,
Professed the disinheriting of your son?
Perjured yourself? Go home, and die, and stink;
If you but croak a syllable, all comes out. 75
Away and call your porters, go, go, stink.

Exit CORBACCIO

VOLPONE (*Aside*)
Excellent varlet!
VOLTORE Now, my faithful Mosca,
I find thy constancy –
MOSCA Sir?
VOLTORE Sincere.
MOSCA A table
Of porphyry – I mar'l, you'll be thus troublesome.

249

84 *travails* efforts. Mosca seems civil to the advocate but this is simply to add salt to his wounds. He will later offer to hire him should he need a lawyer.

96 **Conceive me, for your fee** you can count on me to pay your fee. This is designed to infuriate Voltore because he has 'donated' much of the wealth Mosca now enjoys.

99 *for my plate* the first gift we saw donated.

101 **costive** constipated. The lawyer is obviously puce with fury and leaves. However, ominously, Mosca has been unable to threaten him with blackmail so his threat is by no means removed.

102 **lettuce** a laxative.

105 **clarissimo** nobleman; grandee.

107 **We must pursue** Volpone has become too rapt by his own plotting and now will over-reach himself. Once out of his lair, and thus out of sight of Mosca, he will be vulnerable.

108 *I doubt ... them* Mosca is rapidly becoming disillusioned with the scheme as he believes it will mean an end to their acquisition of wealth.

109 *my recovery ... all* Volpone counters this by saying that he intends to put out soon that he is still alive. Then his suitors will come rushing back.

VOLTORE

Nay, leave off now, they are gone.

MOSCA   Why, who are you?   80
What, who did send for you? O, cry you mercy,
Reverend sir! good faith, I am grieved for you,
That any chance of mine should thus defeat
Your (I must needs say) most deserving travails.
But, I protest, sir, it was cast upon me,   85
And I could, almost, wish to be without it,
But that the will o'the dead must be observed.
Marry, my joy is, that you need it not,
You have a gift, sir (thank your education)
Will never let you want, while there are men,   90
And malice, to breed causes. Would I had
But half the like, for all my fortune, sir.
If I have any suits (as I do hope,
Things being so easy and direct, I shall not)
I will make bold with your obstreperous aid –   95
Conceive me, for your fee, sir. In meantime,
You, that have so much law, I know ha' the conscience
Not to be covetous of what is mine.
Good sir, I thank you for my plate – 'twill help
To set up a young man. Good faith, you look   100
As you were costive; best go home and purge, sir.

Exit VOLTORE

VOLPONE (*Coming out*)

Bid him eat lettuce well. My witty mischief,
Let me embrace thee. O, that I could now
Transform thee to a Venus – Mosca, go,
Straight, take my habit of *clarissimo*,   105
And walk the streets; be seen, torment 'em more;
We must pursue, as well as plot. Who would
Have lost this feast?

MOSCA   I doubt it will lose them.

VOLPONE

O, my recovery shall recover all.

114 **commandadori** officers of the court.

115 *habit* uniform.

116 *answering thy brain* fitting thy intelligence. This is ironic as the uniform allows Mosca, at a stroke, to put Volpone below him on the social scale, and thus less likely to get justice when he moves against him.

119 *The Fox ... cursed* the fox is doomed when he escapes. An ironic use of the proverb: Volpone's escape from the law courts will prove to be a curse as it has led him to risk all.

4 *To Zant, or to Aleppo?* To Zante, a Greek island belonging to Venice at the time, or Aleppo, a city in Syria.

5–6 **Book of Voyages ... truth?** amongst many published travellers' tales, Hakluyt's collection was the most popular. Peregrine comments that Sir Politic could contribute his fantastical stories to it and get them accepted as truth.

That I could now but think on some disguise 110
To meet 'em in, and ask 'em questions.
How I would vex 'em still, at every turn!

MOSCA

Sir, I can fit you.

VOLPONE   Canst thou?

MOSCA   Yes, I know
One o' the *commandadori*, sir, so like you;
Him will I straight make drunk, and bring you his
    habit. 115

VOLPONE

A rare disguise, and answering thy brain!
O, I will be a sharp disease unto 'em.

MOSCA

Sir, you must look for curses –

VOLPONE   Till they burst;
The Fox fares ever best when he is cursed.

Exeunt

Scene four

SIR POLITIC WOULD-BE'S *House*
Enter PEREGRINE *disguised, and three* MERCHANTS

PEREGRINE

Am I enough disguised?

1st MERCHANT   I warrant you.

PEREGRINE

All my ambition is to fright him only.

2nd MERCHANT

If you could ship him away, 'twere excellent.

3rd MERCHANT

To Zant, or to Aleppo?

PEREGRINE   Yes, and ha' his
Adventures put i' th' *Book of Voyages*, 5
And his gulled story registered for truth?

7 *when I am in a while* when I have been inside for some time.

14 *I see ... here* the fact that Sir Politic has a female servant convinces Peregrine that he is a bawd.

18 *exact* force out.

22 *One o' th' ingredients* i.e. to make a greater profit. Peregrine pours scorn on the notion of Sir Politic being involved in affairs of state and, in fact, it turns out he has been writing an apology to his wife.

Well, gentlemen, when I am in a while,
And that you think us warm in our discourse,
Know your approaches.

1st MERCHANT   Trust it to our care.

Exeunt MERCHANTS

Enter WAITING WOMAN

PEREGRINE

Save you, fair lady. Is Sir Pol within?   10

WOMAN

I do not know, sir.

PEREGRINE   Pray you, say unto him,
Here is a merchant, upon earnest business,
Desires to speak with him,

WOMAN   I will see, sir.

PEREGRINE   Pray you.

(*Exit* WOMAN)

I see the family is all female here.

Enter WAITING WOMAN

WOMAN

He says, sir, he has weighty affairs of state   15
That now require him whole – some other time
You may possess him.

PEREGRINE   Pray you, say again,
If those require him whole, these will exact him,
Whereof I bring him tidings. (*Exit* WOMAN)
    What might be
His grave affair of state now? – how to make   20
Bolognian sausages here in Venice, sparing
One o' th' ingredients.

Enter WAITING WOMAN

WOMAN   Sir, he says, he knows
By your word 'tidings' that you are no statesman,
And therefore wills you stay.

PEREGRINE   Sweet, pray you
    return him:
I have not read so many proclamations,   25

35 **punk** prostitute. He still believes his wife's accusation.

38 **To sell Venice ... Turk** a reference back to a throwaway boast of
Sir Politic's in Act 4, scene 1.

41–2 **notes ... play-books** Sir Politic's 'papers', mentioned in the same scene, turn
out to be nothing more than extracts taken from playscripts. His
pomposity is pricked as humiliation piles upon humiliation.

45 **a frail** a sugar chest (like a tea-chest), used by merchants for transporting
sugar.

46–7 **I but talked ... merely** Peregrine's plan goes better than he hoped as here
the knight is forced to recognise his own folly.

And studied them for words, as he has done,
But – Here he deigns to come.

Exit WOMAN

Enter SIR POLITIC WOULD-BE

SIR POLITIC   Sir, I must crave
Your courteous pardon. There hath chanced today
Unkind disaster 'twixt my lady and me,
And I was penning my apology   30
To give her satisfaction, as you came now.

PEREGRINE
Sir, I am grieved I bring you worse disaster;
The gentleman you met at th' port today,
That told you he was newly arrived –

SIR POLITIC   Ay, was
A fugitive punk?

PEREGRINE   No, sir, a spy, set on you;   35
And he has made relation to the Senate
That you professed to him to have a plot
To sell the state of Venice to the Turk.

SIR POLITIC
O me!

PEREGRINE For which, warrants are signed by this time,
To apprehend you, and to search your study   40
For papers –

SIR POLITIC   Alas, sir. I have none but notes
Drawn out of play-books –

PEREGRINE   All the better, sir.

SIR POLITIC
And some essays. What shall I do?

PEREGRINE   Sir, best
Convey yourself into a sugar-chest –
Or, if you could lie round, a frail were rare –   45
And I could send you aboard.

SIR POLITIC   Sir, I but talked so
For discourse sake merely.

They knock without

49 ***currant-butt***   a fruit cask.

50 ***sudden***   quick.

51 ***engine***   device. It turns out to be a tortoise shell in which he hides himself.
The device is so ludicrous as to weaken the play, and has been subjected
to critical scorn throughout the ages. However, it cannot be removed
from the play without damaging it, as all must pay for their vices. Without
this scene, the audience would not learn of the fate of either of the
Would-bes.

PEREGRINE   Hark, they are there.
SIR POLITIC
  I am a wretch, a wretch.
PEREGRINE   What will you do, sir?
  Ha' you ne'er a currant-butt to leap into?
  They'll put you to the rack, you must be sudden.   50
SIR POLITIC
  Sir, I have an engine –
3rd MERCHANT (*Off-stage*) Sir Politic Would-be!
2nd MERCHANT (*Off-stage*)
  Where is he?
SIR POLITIC   – that I have thought upon before time.
PEREGRINE
  What is it?
SIR POLITIC (I shall ne'er endure the torture).
  Marry, it is, sir, of a tortoise-shell,
  Fitted for these extremities: pray you sir, help me.   55
  Here I've a place, sir, to put back my legs –
  Please you to lay it on, sir; with this cap,
  And my black gloves, I'll lie, sir, like a tortoise,
  Till they are gone.
PEREGRINE   And call you this an engine?
SIR POLITIC
  Mine own device – good sir, bid my wife's women   60
  To burn my papers.

                                        Exit PEREGRINE

The MERCHANTS *rush in*
1st MERCHANT   Where's he hid?
3rd MERCHANT   We must,
  And will, sure, find him.
2nd MERCHANT   Which is his study?
Re-enter PEREGRINE
1st MERCHANT   What
  Are you, sir?
PEREGRINE   I'm a merchant, that came here
  To look upon this tortoise.

                                                      259

66 **Nay, you may ... him** ostensibly Peregrine is supporting Sir Politic's disguise but he is really getting the merchants to beat him.

3rd MERCHANT   How?

1st MERCHANT   St Mark!

What beast is this?

PEREGRINE   It is a fish.

2nd MERCHANT   Come out here.   65

PEREGRINE

Nay, you may strike him, sir, and tread upon him –
He'll bear a cart.

1st MERCHANT   What, to run over him?

PEREGRINE   Yes.

3rd MERCHANT

Let's jump upon him.

2nd MERCHANT   Can he not go?

PEREGRINE   He creeps, sir.

1st MERCHANT

Let's see him creep.

Prods him with his sword

PEREGRINE   No, good sir, you will hurt him.

2nd MERCHANT

Heart, I'll see him creep, or prick his guts.   70

3rd MERCHANT

Come out here.

PEREGRINE (*Aside to* SIR POLITIC)

Pray you sir, creep a little.

1st MERCHANT   Forth.

2nd MERCHANT

Yet further.

PEREGRINE (*To* SIR POLITIC) Good sir, Creep.

2nd MERCHANT   We'll see his

legs.

They pull off the shell and discover him

3rd MERCHANT

God's so –, he has garters!

1st MERCHANT   Ay, and gloves!

2nd MERCHANT   Is this

Your fearful tortoise?

76 **funeral of your notes**   Sir Politic has obviously contrived to have his papers burned.

77 **motion**   puppet show.

Fleet Street   meaning the area round the law courts.

78 **i' the term**   whilst the courts were sitting. (At this time the area would be at its busiest and so attract side-shows.)

Smithfield   site of the great fair on St Bartholomew's Day, 24 August.

82–4 **the fable ... ordinaries**   Sir Politic fears public ridicule, saying that he will be the subject of conversations at meals, in the newspapers, on merchant ships and, worst of all, in common taverns. He clearly has not lost all of his pomposity as he again overstates the interest his fall will arouse.

86 **physic**   a cure. Because their crimes are comparatively minor, the pair are punished more gently than the others: they have hurt no one but themselves.

88–9 **Creeping ... shell**   Sir Politic leaves the play a chastened man. He finds the tortoise allusion fitting and, using it, now vows to keep himself to himself; to act with greater prudence.

PEREGRINE (*Removing his disguise*) Now, Sir Pol, we are
  even;
  For your next project, I shall be prepared –   75
  I am sorry for the funeral of your notes, sir.
1st MERCHANT
  'Twere a rare motion to be seen in Fleet Street!
2nd MERCHANT
  Ay, i' the term.
1st MERCHANT   Or Smithfield, in the fair.
3rd MERCHANT
  Methinks 'tis but a melancholic sight!
PEREGRINE
  Farewell, most politic tortoise.

                     Exeunt PEREGRINE, MERCHANTS

Re-enter WAITING WOMAN
SIR POLITIC   Where's my lady?   80
  Knows she of this?
WOMAN   I know not, sir.
SIR POLITIC   Enquire

                          (*Exit* WOMAN)

  O, I shall be the fable of all feasts;
  The freight of the *gazetti*; ship-boys' tale;
  And, which is worst, even talk for ordinaries.
Re-enter WAITING WOMAN
WOMAN
  My lady's come most melancholic home,   85
  And says, sir, she will straight to sea, for physic.
SIR POLITIC
  And I, to shun this place and clime for ever,
  Creeping, with house on back; and think it well,
  To shrink my poor head in my politic shell.

                          Exeunt

4–5 **If I hold ... be well**   now Mosca responds to Volpone in the double-edged
way he has spoken to the legacy-hunters. Ostensibly he means he will do
well if he can keep up the pretence; he also is wondering if he can hold on
to the position he has now found himself in.

6–9 **My Fox ... with me**   my fox is out of his hole and I will make him stay in his
disguise if he does not do a deal with me.

11 **Go, recreate yourselves ...**   the servants are sent out so that Mosca may lock
the house up against Volpone's return: like a fox, he will be kept in the
field by the hunter until he is captured.

13 **needs be**   insist upon.

16–17 **To cozen ... placed**   he deserves to be cheated of all.

18 **Let his sport pay for 't**   let him pay the price of his entertainment.

Scene five

VOLPONE's *House*
Enter VOLPONE, MOSCA; *the first, in the habit of a* commandadore, *the other, of a* clarissimo.

VOLPONE
  Am I then like him?

MOSCA   O, sir, you are he;
  No man can sever you.

VOLPONE   Good.

MOSCA   But what am I?

VOLPONE
  'Fore heaven, a brave *clarissimo*, thou becom'st it!
  Pity thou wert not born one.

MOSCA   If I hold
  My made one, 'twill be well.

VOLPONE   I'll go and see   5
  What news, first, at the court.

Exit VOLPONE   *Exit* VOLPONE

MOSCA   Do so. My Fox
  Is out on his hole, and ere he shall re-enter,
  I'll make him languish in his borrowed case,
  Except he come to composition with me.
  Androgyno, Castrone, Nano!

Enter ANDROGYNO, CASTRONE, NANO

ALL   Here.   10

MOSCA
  Go, recreate yourselves abroad; go, sport.

                    (*Exeunt the three*)
  So, now I have the keys, and am possessed.
  Since he will needs be dead afore his time,
  I'll bury him, or gain by him. I'm his heir,
  And so will keep me, till he share at least.   15
  To cozen him of all were but a cheat
  Well placed; no man would cònstrue it a sin –
  Let his sport pay for't. This is called the Fox-trap.

                       Exit

1–2 **We must ... reputations**   initially we see the plight of Corvino and Corbaccio
       – how to get legal redress without showing themselves guilty of perjury
       and worse.

   5 **come upon him**   make a claim on him. Corbaccio will attempt to prove that
       he changed his will as part of a reciprocal agreement.

Scene six

Near the Scrutineo. Enter CORBACCIO *and* CORVINO

CORBACCIO

They say the court is set.

CORVINO   We must maintain

Our first tale good, for both our reputations.

CORBACCIO

Why? mine's no tale. My son would there have killed
 me.

CORVINO

That's true, I had forgot; mine is, I am sure.

But for your will, sir.

CORBACCIO   Ay, I'll come upon him   5

For that hereafter, now his patron's dead.

Enter VOLPONE *disguised*

VOLPONE

Signior Corvino! and Corbaccio! sir,

Much joy unto you.

CORVINO   Of what?

VOLPONE   The sudden good

Dropped down upon you –

CORBACCIO   Where?

VOLPONE   And none knows how –

From old Volpone, sir.

CORBACCIO   Out, arrant knave.   10

VOLPONE

Let not your too much wealth, sir, make you furious.

CORBACCIO

Away, thou varlet.

VOLPONE   Why sir?

CORBACCIO   Dost thou mock me?

VOLPONE

You mock the world, sir; did you not change wills?

CORBACCIO

Out, harlot.

VOLPONE O! belike you are the man,

17–19 **You are not ... autumn**   Volpone torments Corvino by pretending that he has heard the latter has been announced the heir to the fortune. He compliments him on not becoming puffed up by his harvest of riches.

21 **a very woman**   i.e. inconstant. Again he brings up the previous case to aggravate Corvino.

23 **To bear it out**   to put up with it.

2 **and make legs, for crumbs**   Voltore is furious not only that he has been cheated but that it has been done by one so low.

7 **I mean to be ... worship**   Volpone again teases the disappointed, this time by asking if he can become the lawyer's tenant and naming one of the properties from the will.

Signior Corvino? Faith, you carry it well;   15
You grow not mad withal; I love your spirit.
You are not over-leavened with your fortune.
You should ha' some would swell now like a wine-fat
With such an autumn – Did he gi' you all, sir?

CORVINO

Avoid, you rascal.

VOLPONE   Troth, your wife has shown   20
Herself a very woman; but you are well,
You need not care, you have a good estate
To bear it out, sir, better by this chance.
Except Corbaccio have a share . . . ?

CORBACCIO   Hence, varlet.

VOLPONE

You will not be a'known, sir – why, 'tis wise.   25
Thus do all gamesters, at all games, dissemble.
No man will seem to win.

(*Exeunt* CORBACCIO, CORVINO)

Here comes my vulture,
Heaving his beak up i' the air, and snuffing.

(*Scene seven*)

Enter VOLTORE

VOLTORE

Outstripped thus, by a parasite? a slave?
Would run on errands? and make legs, for crumbs?
Well, what I'll do –

VOLPONE   The court stays for your worship.
I e'en rejoice, sir, at your worship's happiness,
And that it fell into so learned hands,   5
That understand the fingering –

VOLTORE   What do you mean?

VOLPONE

I mean to be a suitor to your worship

10 **Piscaria**   fish market.

15 *prating*   chattering.

16 *give me but your hand*   let's shake on it.

17 *the refusal*   first refusal.

18 *candle-rents*   rents from worthless properties.

20 *God decrease it!*   acting as a common man, he pretends to get his words mixed up, using decrease when he means the opposite. He is, of course, expressing a genuine sentiment.

23 *to my first again*   to my first victims again. Volpone is enjoying his ruse but is blind to the harm it is doing. In particular, it will convince Voltore that he has nothing to lose by making a clean breast of things to the judges.

1 *our habit*   either, dressed like one of us (a noble); or, dressed in the clothes which should be ours.

For the small tenement, out of reparations –
That at the end of your long row of houses,
By the *Piscaria*; it was, in Volpone's time,   10
Your predecessor, ere he grew diseased,
A handsome, pretty, customed bawdy-house
As any was in Venice (none dispraised),
But fell with him; his body and that house
Decayed together.

VOLTORE   Come, sir, leave your prating.   15

VOLPONE

Why, if your worship give me but your hand,
That I may ha' the refusal, I have done.
'Tis a mere toy to you, sir – candle-rents.
As your learn'd worship knows –

VOLTORE   What do I know?

VOLPONE

Marry, no end of your wealth, sir, God decrease it!   20

VOLTORE

Mistaking knave! what, mock'st thou my misfortune?

VOLPONE

His blessing on your heart, sir, would 'twere more.

                              (*Exit* VOLTORE)

– Now, to my first again; at the next corner.

                              Stands aside

Scene eight

Enter CORBACCIO, CORVINO, (MOSCA *passant*)

CORBACCIO

See, in our habit! see the impudent varlet!

CORVINO

That I could shoot mine eyes at him, like gunstones!

VOLPONE (*Stepping forward*)

But is this true, sir, of the parasite?

6 ***over-reached*** outsmarted.

  never brooked never liked.

9 ***bane*** ruin.

10–14 ***Yet you ... emptiness*** Volpone again refers to the fable of the fox and the crow. His intention is to bait them but he is going a little too far by suggesting the fox was behind their fall if indeed he plans to 'rise from the dead'. His over-confidence has made him reckless and it is he who, ironically, is in danger of being cheated by his singing.

13 ***sung your shame*** i.e. declared yourself a cuckold.

16–17 ***red, saucy cap ... chequeens*** Corbaccio refers to the headdress of the officer of the state. He mentions its colour and the buttons on its side, which look like gold coins. He warns Volpone that the uniform will not save him from punishment.

21 ***durst publish what you are*** again Volpone taunts Corvino with his self-humiliation.

CORBACCIO

    Again, t'afflict us? monster!

VOLPONE   In good faith, sir,

    I'm heartily grieved, a beard of your grave length   5

    Should be so over-reached. I never brooked

    That parasite's hair, methought his nose should cozen;

    There still was somewhat in his look did promise

    The bane of a *clarissimo*.

CORBACCIO   Knave –

VOLPONE   Methinks

    Yet you, that are so traded i' the world,   10

    A witty merchant, the fine bird, Corvino,

    That have such moral emblems on your name,

    Should not have sung your shame, and dropped your

      cheese,

    To let the Fox laugh at your emptiness.

CORVINO

    Sirrah, you think the privilege of the place,   15

    And your red, saucy cap, that seems, to me,

    Nailed to your jolt-head with those two chequeens,

    Can warrant your abuses; come you hither –

    You shall perceive, sir, I dare beat you. Approach.

VOLPONE

    No haste, sir, I do know your valour well,   20

    Since you durst publish what you are, sir.

CORVINO   Tarry,

    I'd speak with you.

VOLPONE   Sir, sir, another time –

CORVINO

    Nay, now.

VOLPONE   O God, sir! I were a wise man,

    Would stand the fury of a distracted cuckold.

                                Mosca walks by 'em

CORBACCIO

    What! come again?

VOLPONE   Upon 'em, Mosca; save me.   25

27 **basilisk** a reptile which was fabled to be able to kill with a look.

 I **flesh-fly** a blow-fly lays its eggs in corpses. The image equates Mosca with the other legacy-hunters.

 4 **'solecism'** public impropriety.

 5 **biggin** a lawyer's cap.

10 **Justinian** the emperor who created the Roman legal code.

11 **quirk** trick.

14 **This's but ... rest** taking advantage of what he has heard, Volpone now throws the lawyer's early hope about Mosca's behaviour in his face. This is intended to madden him more.

CORBACCIO
  The air's infected where he breathes.
CORVINO   Let's fly him.
                              Exeunt CORBACCIO, CORVINO

VOLPONE
  Excellent basilisk! turn upon the vulture.

(*Scene nine*)

Enter VOLTORE

VOLTORE
  Well, flesh-fly, it is summer with you now;
  Your winter will come on.
MOSCA   Good advocate,
  Pray thee not rail, nor threaten out of place, thus;
  Thou'lt make a 'solecism', as madam says.
  Get you a biggin more – your brain breaks loose.   5
                                                         Exit

VOLTORE
  Well, sir.
VOLPONE   Would you ha' me beat the insolent slave?
  Throw dirt upon his first good clothes?
VOLTORE   This same
  Is doubtless some familiar!
VOLPONE   Sir, the court,
  In troth, stays for you. I am mad, a mule
  That never read Justinian should get up   10
  And ride an advocate. Had you no quirk
  To avoid gullage, sir, by such a creature?
  I hope you do but jest; he has not done't;
  This's but confederacy, to blind the rest.
  You are the heir?
VOLTORE   A strange, officious,   15
  Troublesome knave! thou dost torment me.
VOLPONE   I know –

17 **cozened**   tricked.

4 **Once win upon**   for once overcome your ruling. Voltore has decided to cut
   his losses and confess, claiming he was falsely advised. The taunting of
   Volpone and the pomposity of Mosca have driven him to this.

9 **most covetous ends**   for reasons of pure greed.

It cannot be, sir, that you should be cozened;
'Tis not within the wit of man to do it,
You are so wise, so prudent – and 'tis fit
That wealth and wisdom still should go together.   20

Exeunt

Scene ten

The Scrutineo
Enter four AVOCATORI, NOTARIO, COMMANDADORI, BONARIO, CELIA,
CORBACCIO, CORVINO

1st AVOCATORE
  Are all the parties here?
NOTARIO   All but the advocate.
2nd AVOCATORE
  And here he comes.
Enter VOLTORE, VOLPONE
1st AVOCATORE   Then bring 'em forth to sentence.
                              BONARIO, CELIA *are led forward*
VOLTORE O, my most honoured fathers, let your mercy
  Once win upon your justice, to forgive –
  I am distracted –
VOLPONE (*Aside*)   What will he do now?
VOLTORE   O,   5
  I know not which t'address myself to first,
  Whether your fatherhoods, or these innocents –
CORVINO (*Aside*)
  Will he betray himself?
VOLTORE   – whom, equally,
  I have abused, out of most covetous ends –
CORVINO (*To* CORBACCIO)
  The man is mad!
CORBACCIO   What's that?
CORVINO   He is possessed.   10

277

13–14 ***I'm caught I' mine own noose***   as another crisis looms, Volpone realises that he has trapped himself by naming Mosca as his heir and then taunting the others. He has over-reached himself because his latest scheme had no definable profit attached to it, being simply to satisfy a whim.

16–18 ***It is not passion ... truth***   the irony is, of course, that Voltore could not make this plea if he did have a conscience. He speaks only out of disappointed greed.

VOLTORE

    For which, now struck in conscience, here I prostrate
    Myself at your offended feet, for pardon.

1st and 2nd AVOCATORI

    Arise.

CELIA   O Heaven, how just thou art!

VOLPONE (*Aside*)   I'm caught

    I' mine own noose –

CORVINO (*To* CORBACCIO) Be constant, sir; naught now
    Can help but impudence.

1st AVOCATORE   Speak forward.

COMMANDADORE   Silence!   15

VOLTORE

    It is not passion in me, reverend fathers,
    But only conscience, conscience, my good sires,
    That makes me now tell truth. That parasite,
    That knave, hath been the instrument of all.

1st AVOCATORE

    Where is that knave? fetch him.

VOLPONE   I go.

                            Exit VOLPONE

CORVINO   Grave fathers,   20

    This man's distracted; he confessed it now;
    For, hoping to be old Volpone's heir,
    Who now is dead –

3rd AVOCATORE   How?

2nd AVOCATORE   Is Volpone dead?

CORVINO

    Dead since, grave fathers –

BONARIO   O, sure vengeance!

1st AVOCATORE   Stay –

    Then he was no deceiver?

VOLTORE   O no, none;   25

    The parasite, grave fathers.

CORVINO   He does speak

    Out of mere envy, 'cause the servant's made

28   *gaped*   again a reference back to Aesop's fable and again greed is associated with hunger.

30   **The other ... faulty**   i.e. Mosca. Corvino is trying to have it both ways and thus confusing the proceedings. He claims Voltore is speaking nonsense except for the notion that Mosca has done something wrong.

35   **The devil ... him!**   it is indicative of the moral values prevalent in Venice that when a man actually does speak the truth he is accused of being possessed.

36–7   **We have done ... heir**   once again social position rather than the scope of a potential crime is the major concern.

44   *my fame – Where is't?*   Corvino pleads for his reputation and Bonario points out that he has already given this away. He is referring to the former's attempt to prostitute his wife.

The thing he gaped for; please your fatherhoods,
This is the truth; though I'll not justify
The other, but he may be some-deal faulty.   30
VOLTORE

Ay, to your hopes, as well as mine, Corvino.
But I'll use modesty. Pleaseth your wisdoms
To view these certain notes, and but confer them;

(Gives them papers)

As I hope favour, they shall speak clear truth.
CORVINO

The devil has entered him!
BONARIO   Or bides in you.   35
4th AVOCATORE

We have done ill, by a public officer
To send for him, if he be heir.
2nd AVOCATORE   For whom?
4th AVOCATORE

Him that they call the parasite.
3rd AVOCATORE   'Tis true;

He is a man of great estate now left.
4th AVOCATORE

Go you, and learn his name; and say the court   40
Entreats his presence here, but to the clearing
Of some few doubts.

Exit NOTARIO

2nd AVOCATORE   This same's a labyrinth!
1st AVOCATORE

Stand you unto your first report?
CORVINO   My state,

My life, my fame –
BONARIO   Where is't?
CORVINO   – are at the stake.
1st AVOCATORE

Is yours so too?
CORBACCIO   The advocate's a knave,   45
And has a forkèd tongue –

47 **So is the parasite, too** again confusion is added by the attempt to discredit Voltore but implicate Mosca. The stupidity of Corvino and Corbaccio contrasts strongly with the skilled plotting of Volpone and Mosca.

2 **with laughter** simply to amuse myself.

4 **mere wantonness** self-indulgence.

6 **gave it second** agreed to it.

7 **Help to sear up ... bleed** help to put right this injury or we are finished. It is interesting to note that Volpone sees their fates as intertwined. The meeting with his bastard offspring will make him realise how wrong he is.

9 **ginger-bread? ... kitlings?** in Volpone's perverted scale of values the two are interchangeable in terms of seriousness. They are both accepted practices.

13–14 **I am farther in ... to me!** the lines show how quickly Volpone bounces back. Mosca's actions in sending out the servants makes him suspect for the first time how dire his situation is. By the next line he has accepted the mess is of his own making and has determined to enjoy himself.

2nd AVOCATORE   Speak to the point.

CORBACCIO

    So is the parasite, too.

1st AVOCATORE   This is confusion.

VOLTORE

    I do beseech your fatherhoods, read but those.

Indicating his notes

CORVINO

    And credit nothing the false spirit hath writ.

    It cannot be but he is possessed, grave fathers.   50

Exeunt

Scene eleven

A Street

Enter VOLPONE

VOLPONE

    To make a snare for mine own neck! and run

    My head into it wilfully! with laughter!

    When I had newly scaped, was free and clear!

    Out of mere wantonness! O, the dull devil

    Was in this brain of mine when I devised it,   5

    And Mosca gave it second; he must now

    Help to sear up this vein, or we bleed dead.

(*Enter* NANO, ANDROGYNO, CASTRONE)

    How now! who let you loose? whither go you now?

    What, to buy ginger-bread? or to drown kitlings?

NANO

    Sir, master Mosca called us out of doors,   10

    And bid us all go play, and took the keys.

ANDROGYNO   Yes.

VOLPONE

    Did master Mosca take the keys? why, so!

    I am farther in. These are my fine conceits!

    I must be merry, with a mischief to me!

18   **His meaning ... fear**   the reason he can be so bold is that he remembers
Mosca's warning in Act 3, scene 8 (lines 20–1) that things are often not as
black as we perceive them to be. He has convinced himself that Mosca
does not intend to betray him.

1   **can ne'er be reconciled**   this is explained a little later. Voltore only knows
what Mosca has told him. Therefore, he now testifies that Corvino
intended to prostitute Celia to Volpone but that the latter could not
ravish her because he was impotent with illness: the scheme, therefore,
seems too absurd to be true, particularly as Corvino has publicly
pronounced himself a cuckold by another man.

9–10   **possession and obsession**   'possession' was to have demons controlling you
from within, 'obsession', from without.

What a vile wretch was I, that could not bear   15
My fortune soberly! I must ha' my crotchets!
And my conundrums! well, go you and seek him –
His meaning may be truer than my fear.
Bid him, he straight come to me, to the court;
Thither will I, and, if't be possible,   20
Unscrew my advocate, upon new hopes.
When I provoked him, then I lost myself.

Exeunt

Scene twelve

The Scrutineo

Four AVOCATORI, VOLTORE, BONARIO, CELIA, CORBACCIO,
CORVINO, COMMANDADORI

1st AVOCATORE

These things can ne'er be reconciled. He, here,
                      (*Indicating* VOLTORE'S *papers*)
Professeth that the gentleman was wronged;
And that the gentlewoman was brought thither,
Forced by her husband, and there left.

VOLTORE   Most true.

CELIA

How ready is Heaven to those that pray!

1st AVOCATORE   But that   5
Volpone would have ravished her, he holds
Utterly false, knowing his impotence.

CORVINO

Grave fathers, he is possessed; again, I say,
Possessed; nay, if there be possession
And obsession, he has both.

3rd AVOCATORE   Here comes our officer.   10

Enter VOLPONE

12 **invent some other name**   i.e. because he now has rank he should not be
denigrated.

20 **Do I live, sir?**   an intended irony.

24–8 **See, see ... his belly**   the description is partly to convince the judges that
Voltore is possessed, partly to tell the advocate how to act the part.

VOLPONE

The parasite will straight be here, grave fathers.

4th AVOCATORE

You might invent some other name, sir varlet.

3rd AVOCATORE

Did not the notary meet him?

VOLPONE   Not that I know.

4th AVOCATORE

His coming will clear all.

2nd AVOCATORE   Yet, it is misty.

VOLTORE

May't please your fatherhoods –

                              VOLPONE *whispers to the advocate*

VOLPONE   Sir, the parasite   15
Willed me to tell you that his master lives;
That you are still the man; your hopes, the same;
And this was only a jest –

VOLTORE   How?

VOLPONE   Sir, to try
If you were firm, and how you stood affected.

VOLTORE

Art sure he lives?

VOLPONE   Do I live, sir?

VOLTORE   O me!   20
I was too violent.

VOLPONE   Sir, you may redeem it –
They said, you were possessed; fall down, and seem so;
I'll help to make it good. (VOLTORE *falls*) God bless the
    man!
(*To* VOLTORE) Stop your wind hard, and swell – See, see,
    see, see!
He vomits crooked pins! his eyes are set,   25
Like a dead hare's hung in a poulter's shop!
His mouth's running away! do you see, signior?
Now, 'tis in his belly.

32–3 ***What? I think ... manifest*** their responses show that they have no concept of the truth.

35 ***dispossessed*** freed from possession (see note to lines 9–10).

CORVINO   Ay, the devil!
VOLPONE
  Now, in his throat.
CORVINO   Ay, I perceive it plain.
VOLPONE
  'Twill out, 'twill out; stand clear. See where it flies!   30
  In shape of a blue toad, with a bat's wings!
  Do not you see it, sir?
CORBACCIO   What? I think I do.
CORVINO
  'Tis too manifest.
VOLPONE   Look! he comes t'himself!
VOLTORE
  Where am I?
VOLPONE   Take good heart, the worst is past, sir.
  You are dispossessed.
1st AVOCATORE   What accident is this?   35
2nd AVOCATORE
  Sudden, and full of wonder!
3rd AVOCATORE   If he were
  Possessed, as it appears, all this is nothing.
CORVINO
  He has been often subject to these fits.
1st AVOCATORE
  Show him that writing. Do you know it, sir?
VOLPONE (*Aside to* VOLTORE)
  Deny it, sir, forswear it, know it not.   40
VOLTORE
  Yes, I do know it well, it is my hand;
  But all that it contains is false.
BONARIO   O practice!
2nd AVOCATORE
  What maze is this!
1st AVOCATORE   Is he not guilty then,
  Whom you there name the parasite?

51 **A fit match for my daughter**   in the corrupt world of Venice, even those who dispense justice are on the look-out for ways to make money. One has only to look at how Mosca is initially treated to see which comes first in the scale of priorities, status or justice.

54 **All's o' the hinge again**   everything is all right again.

55–7 **What busy knave ... funeral**   far from going along with the plan, Mosca shuns Volpone in public, instead pronouncing him dead. He will keep this up whilst the two, in a series of asides, barter a price for him to change his tune.

VOLTORE   Grave fathers,
No more than his good patron, old Volpone.   45
4th AVOCATORE
Why, he is dead?
VOLTORE   O no, my honoured fathers.
He lives –
1st AVOCATORE How! lives?
VOLTORE   Lives.
2nd AVOCATORE   This is subtler yet!
You said he was dead!
VOLTORE   Never.
3rd AVOCATORE (*To* CORVINO) You said so!
CORVINO   I heard so.
4th AVOCATORE
Here comes the gentleman; make him way.
Enter MOSCA
3rd AVOCATORE   A stool!
4th AVOCATORE (*Aside*)
A proper man! and were Volpone dead,   50
A fit match for my daughter.
3rd AVOCATORE   Give him way.
VOLPONE (*Aside to* MOSCA)
Mosca, I was a'most lost; the advocate
Had betrayed all; but now it is recovered.
All's o' the hinge again – say I am living.
MOSCA
What busy knave is this! Most reverend fathers,   55
I sooner had attended your grave pleasures,
But that my order for the funeral
Of my dear patron did require me –
VOLPONE (*Aside*)   Mosca!
MOSCA
Whom I intend to bury like a gentleman.
VOLPONE (*Aside*)
Ay, quick, and cozen me of all.

64 **cry not so loud**   Volpone, in his anger, is beginning to speak too loudly.

69–70 **I cannot ... cheap**   having named his price and got it easily, Mosca realises his power and demands more. He has failed to learn the lesson about greed he has taught the others and now over-reaches himself. It is foolish of him to think that one who enjoys victory as much as Volpone, will accept defeat, and a consequent whipping, gracefully.

74 **I was born ... enemies**   I was born to be a fool of Fortune.

2nd AVOCATORE   Still stranger!   60
  More intricate!
1st AVOCATORE   And come about again!
4th AVOCATORE (*Aside*)
  It is a match, my daughter is bestowed.
MOSCA (*Aside to* VOLPONE)
  Will you gi' me half?
VOLPONE (*Aside to* MOSCA) First, I'll be hanged.
MOSCA (*Aside to* VOLPONE)   I know
  Your voice is good; cry not so loud.
1st AVOCATORE   Demand
  The advocate. Sir, did not you affirm   65
  Volpone was alive?
VOLPONE   Yes, and he is;
  This gent'man (*Indicating* MOSCA) told me so.
  (*Aside to* MOSCA)   Thou shalt have half.
MOSCA
  Whose drunkard is this same? speak some that know
    him –
  I never saw his face. (*Aside to* VOLPONE) I cannot now
  Afford it you so cheap.
VOLPONE (*Aside to* MOSCA) No?
1st AVOCATORE   What say you?   70
VOLTORE
  The officer told me.
VOLPONE   I did, grave fathers,
  And will maintain he lives, with mine own life,
  And (*Indicating* MOSCA) that this creature told me.
  (*Aside*)   I was born
  With all good stars my enemies.
MOSCA   Most grave fathers,
  If such an insolence as this must pass   75
  Upon me, I am silent; 'twas not this
  For which you sent, I hope.
2nd AVOCATORE   Take him away.

78 **Let him be whipped**   in his guise as a common man, Volpone can be
subjected to punishments fitting to that class. The punishment, and the
reason for it, makes Volpone realise how low he has sunk, and he begins
to weigh up the price of disclosure of his true identity.

84 **They'll be allied anon**   the marital plans of the 4th Avocatore mean that he
has to act quickly if he is to have legal redress. It is assumed that no one
will take action against a judge's son-in-law, a fact which confirms the
audience's view of Venetian justice.

84 **Patron!**   this is said as an aside to Volpone. Mosca sees that he is ruined and
immediately reverts to his original status. His aim is to bargain for his life
but he is ignored.

88 **a family**   i.e. of good name.

89–91 **I am ... and knave**   Volpone now unmasks all, revealing Voltore as a dupe,
Corbaccio as a victim of his own greed and, with most scorn, Corvino as a
monstrous combination of a pimp, fool and cuckold.

VOLPONE (*Aside*)
  Mosca!
3rd AVOCATORE
        Let him be whipped –
VOLPONE (*Aside*)   Wilt thou betray me?
  Cozen me?
3rd AVOCATORE – and taught to bear himself
  Toward a person of his rank.
4th AVOCATORE   Away.   80

                              VOLPONE *is seized*

MOSCA
  I humbly thank your fatherhoods.
VOLPONE (*Aside*)   Soft, soft. Whipped?
  And lose all that I have? if I confess,
  It cannot be much more.
4th AVOCATORE (*To* MOSCA) Sir, are you married?
VOLPONE
  They'll be allied anon; I must be resolute:

                              (*He puts off his disguise*)

  The fox shall here uncase.
MOSCA (*Aside*)   Patron!
VOLPONE   Nay, now   85
  My ruins shall not come alone; your match
  I'll hinder sure; my substance shall not glue you,
  Nor screw you, into a family.
MOSCA (*Aside*)   Why, patron!
VOLPONE
  I am Volpone, and this (*Pointing to* MOSCA) is my
    knave;
  This, (*To* VOLTORE) his own knave; this, (*to* CORBACCIO)
    avarice's fool;   90
  This, (*To* CORVINO) a chimera of wittol, fool, and knave;
  And, reverend fathers, since we all can hope
  Naught but a sentence, let's not now despair it.
  You hear me brief.
CORVINO   May it please your fatherhoods –

                              295

98 **Heaven ... be hid** Bonario attributes the destruction of evil to Providence, as is traditional of comedies of this time, but the thrust of the play would seem to be that evil destroyed itself whilst justice stood powerless. The pious words about the curse of wealth which follow from the judges are hardly reassuring, given that one of their number has been trying to set up a marriage beneficial to himself. Like much else in the play, they smack of hypocrisy.

106 **You hurt ... guilty** you cast doubts upon your innocence by pleading for the guilty. Although Celia's plea for mercy is merely Jonson bowing to convention, it is nevertheless a sign of her virtue: the judge shows an alarming blindness to this fact.

107–39 **and first ... berlino** the lines which follow are all fitting to the nature of the crimes committed. Mosca, who had pretensions to be rich and has enjoyed a life of leisure, will be whipped as a peasant and then imprisoned on a galley; Volpone, who sought wealth through feigning illness, will be chained up in a hospital for the incurably ill until he gets one of their diseases and dies; Voltore, who abused his gift of eloquence, will be forbidden to use it to gain a living and is banished from Venice, and thus from folks of his native tongue; Corbaccio, who sought wealth, will have his estate given to his son and will be confined in a monastery to live a life of poverty; and Corvino, who inadvertently sought public humiliation, shall be granted it by being paraded before all Venice as an ass before being stocked.

COMMANDADORE   Silence!
1st AVOCATORE
  The knot is now undone, by miracle!   95
2nd AVOCATORE
  Nothing can be more clear.
3rd AVOCATORE   Or can more prove
  These innocent.
1st AVOCATORE   Give 'em their liberty.
BONARIO
  Heaven could not long let such gross crimes be hid.
2nd AVOCATORE
  If this be held the highway to get riches,
  May I be poor.
3rd AVOCATORE   This's not the gain, but torment.   100
1st AVOCATORE
  These possess wealth, as sick men possess fevers,
  Which, trulier, may be said to possess them.
2nd AVOCATORE
  Disrobe that parasite.
CORVINO, MOSCA   Most honoured fathers –
1st AVOCATORE
  Can you plead aught to stay the course of justice?
  If you can, speak.
CORVINO, VOLTORE We beg favour.
CELIA   And mercy.   105
1st AVOCATORE
  You hurt your innocence, suing for the guilty.
  Stand forth; and first, the parasite. You appear
  T'have been the chiefest minister, if not plotter,
  In all these lewd impostures; and now, lastly,
  Have, with your impudence, abused the court   110
  And habit of a gentleman of Venice,
  Being a fellow of no birth or blood;
  For which, our sentence is, first thou be whipped;
  Then live perpetual prisoner in our galleys.

115 **Bane**   death. Mosca's last words are a vicious pun in that wolf's-bane is another name for aconite, a poisonous plant.

125 *mortifying*   it is fitting that Volpone too should leave with a pun, in that 'mortifying' could mean: killing; subduing by submitting to discipline; or, causing gangrene or tissue death.

139 **berlino**   the pillory.

VOLPONE

    I thank you for him.

MOSCA   Bane to thy wolfish nature.   115

1st AVOCATORE

    Deliver him to the *Saffi*. (MOSCA *is led aside*) Thou, Vol-
       pone,

    By blood and rank a gentleman, canst not fall

    Under like censure; but our judgment on thee

    Is, that thy substance all be straight confiscate

    To the hospital of the *Incurabili*;   120

    And, since the most was gotten by imposture,

    By feigning lame, gout, palsy, and such diseases,

    Thou art to lie in prison, cramped with irons,

    Till thou be'st sick and lame indeed. Remove him.

VOLPONE

    This is called mortifying of a fox.   125

                              VOLPONE *is led aside*

1st AVOCATORE

    Thou, Voltore, to take away the scandal

    Thou hast given all worthy men of thy profession,

    Art banished from their fellowship, and our state.

    Corbaccio! – bring him near. We here possess

    Thy son of all thy state; and confine thee   130

    To the monastery of *San' Spirito*,

    Where, since thou knew'st not how to live well here,

    Thou shalt be learned to die well.

CORBACCIO   Ha! what said he?

COMMANDADORE (*Leading him aside*)

    You shall know anon, sir.

1st AVOCATORE   Thou, Corvino, shalt

    Be straight embarked from thine own house, and rowed   135

    Round about Venice, through the *Grand Canale*,

    Wearing a cap with fair, long ass's ears

    Instead of horns; and so to mount, a paper

    Pinned on thy breast, to the *berlino* –

CORVINO   Yes,

149–50   **Let all ... study 'em**   the judge sums up the purpose of this and other comedies: to expose human vices to laughter, allowing the audience to learn both their nature and that they will always be punished.

152–7   **The seasoning ... hands**   another convention of comedy in which one of the principal players steps out of role to apologise for any offence given and to ask for the audience's applause for the cast.

And have mine eyes beat out with stinking fish,   140
Bruised fruit, and rotten eggs – 'Tis well. I'm glad
I shall not see my shame yet.

1st AVOCATORE   And to expiate
Thy wrongs done to thy wife, thou art to send her
Home, to her father, with her dowry trebled.
And these are all your judgments –

ALL   Honoured fathers!   145

1st AVOCATORE
– which may not be revoked. Now you begin,
When crimes are done, and past, and to be punished,
To think what your crimes are. Away with them!
Let all that see these vices thus rewarded,
Take heart, and love to study 'em. Mischiefs feed   150
Like beasts, till they be fat, and then they bleed.

                                    Exeunt

VOLPONE *comes forward*

VOLPONE
The seasoning of a play is the applause.
Now, though the Fox be punished by the laws,
He yet doth hope there is no suffering due
For any fact which he hath done 'gainst you.   155
If there be, censure him – here he doubtful stands.
If not, fare jovially, and clap your hands.

Study programme

Reading the text

The following questions/tasks are intended to help you interpret the text as you encounter it. If answered in detail, they will provide you with much of the information you need to attempt the essay questions which follow. All can be used as the basis for discussion activities in seminar groups.

The Epistle

1. Jot down the key points Jonson makes, focusing upon:

- his notion of the dramatist's role;
- his criticisms of his contemporary dramatists.

Act I

Scene 1

1. Read lines 1–27. What does the speech show us about the character of Volpone?

2. Read lines 30–65. How do Volpone and Mosca justify their methods for acquiring gold? What pleasures dominate Volpone's life?

Scene 2

3. What do you think is the dramatic purpose of the entertainment? What themes does it introduce to the play?

4 Line 89 marks the beginning of the animal imagery in the play. Create a section in your Reading log and begin to collect examples of this now.

5 Lines 99–114 give Mosca's view of life. What does he understand about it?

6 The exchange between Volpone and Mosca in lines 99–114 gives valuable clues as to the nature of their relationship. How would you describe it?

Scene 3

7 Look carefully at the way that Volpone and Mosca treat Voltore. Why are they so successful in duping him? What evidence is there that they enjoy their swindling?

Scene 4

8 Do you agree that the comedy in this scene is much blacker? Support your opinion with textual evidence.

9 Lines 93–110 show Mosca to be a cunning intriguer. How does he persuade Corbaccio to disinherit his son? Why does the old man fall for it so quickly?

Scene 5

10 What do lines 51–74 show about Mosca's attitude to his patron?

Act I summary questions

1 What are the differences in the way that Mosca plays the three suitors? Are there signs that he is also manipulating his master?

2 What two plot complications are introduced in this Act? Identify each and then follow its development, tracing how it affects our views of Corvino and Corbaccio.

3 A collective in name and motive, the legacy-hunters have been criticised by some critics as being too similar. Do you agree? In preparing your answer, pay particular attention to:

- their attitudes to Volpone's imminent death and how they express them;
- their own personalities;
- their treatment of Mosca.

Act 2

Scene 1

1 What do we learn of Sir Politic in this scene? Peregrine says of his name, 'O, that speaks him' (line 25). Do you agree?

2 Is Peregrine's name fitting considering the role he is to play?

3 How could you edit the scene to make it more intelligible to a modern audience? Would you lose anything in doing so?

Scene 2

4 Why does Volpone speak in prose when he mimics Scoto of Mantua?

5 In this scene Volpone scorns all imitators. As you are reading the play, note other instances when characters make a similar pronouncement. Is there an irony in this?

Scene 5

6. What do we learn of the relationship between Corvino and Celia in this scene? How does this add to our understanding of Corvino's character?

Scene 7

7. Look at Corvino's final speech. What is its impact upon the audience?

Act 2 summary questions

1. How much is Mosca to blame and how much Corvino for the latter's decision to send his wife to Volpone's bed?

2. To what extent are Volpone and Mosca equals? Does Mosca act like a servant or are there signs that he has higher aspirations? Does Volpone encourage these, albeit inadvertently?

3. Flattery is a key element in the relationship between Volpone and Mosca. Look at what they say to each other – is there any love between them or are they simply indulging in hollow compliments?

Act 3

Scene 1

1. How does Mosca justify his role as a parasite? What insights does this give us into his character and how he perceives his relationship with Volpone?

Scene 2

2. Mosca's speech in scene 1 is immediately followed by the scene

in which he encounters Bonario. How does this further illuminate the character of the parasite? What are our first impressions of Bonario?

Scene 4

3 Volpone says of the approach of Lady Would-be:

> *A second hell too, that my loathing this*
> *Will quite expel my appetite to the other.*

Act 3, scene 3, lines 28–9

What are the elements of comedy in the scene which follows?

Scene 7

4 Why is Mosca so distraught to see Corvino? What does his plotting rely upon?

5 Why has Corvino arrived so early? What irony does Mosca see in this?

6 How does Corvino's persuasion of Celia mirror Volpone's attempts to seduce her? How moving is Celia's defence of her honour?

7 How convincing are Volpone's words of love? Why? Does he attract or repel you in this scene?

8 How do you react to Bonario as he saves Celia? To what extent is he a comic figure?

Scene 9

9 This is a scene of great confusion in which all question Mosca's motives. How does he convince each that he serves him only?

10 Volpone says, 'Need makes devotion; Heaven your labour bless' (line 63). Is this a serious sentiment or is he being blasphemous? Where else do we see him speak like this?

Act 3 summary questions

1. How does the scene with Volpone and Lady Would-be mirror his later seduction of Celia?

2. Scene 7 is a tricky one to direct because its tone is ambiguous. Imagine you are the director of a new production and decide how you would approach it.

   Beginning with the arrival of Celia and Corvino make detailed notes for your actors about how you want them to play the scene. Key things to cover are:

   - how speeches should be delivered;
   - how they should move;
   - what their intended effect on the audience is – should they horrify or amuse their spectators?
   - whether Celia is to be a sympathetic creature or not.

   Follow up activities:

   - Compare your notes with others in the group and discuss differing interpretations.
   - Act out two different interpretations and see which works best.

Act 4

Scene 1

1. What do Sir Politic's money-making schemes show about him? Trace each and see how feasible they are.

2. How, as a member of the audience, do you react to this scene? Is it still comic or has it become dated, and therefore tedious? Explain your opinion.

Scene 2

3 This scene sees the play reduced to farce – what misconceptions lead to this chaos? What do we learn about the relationship of Sir Politic and his wife?

Scene 4

4 To what extent does Mosca appear to be in control in this scene? Is he enjoying his power? How do you think the episode will alter the relationship between him and his master?

Scenes 5 and 6

5 The avocatori begin the scene shocked by Volpone's vice yet end the Act by apologising to him and imprisoning Bonario and Celia. What factors lead them to this change of heart?

6 How, as an audience, do we react to Celia and Bonario in the courtroom scene?

Act 4 summary questions

1 In what sense could this Act be said to glorify in the triumph of evil?

2 Would it be a more fitting final act for the play than the existing one? Justify your point of view.

Act 5

Scene 1

1 What frame of mind has the trial put Volpone in?

Scene 2

2 What signs are there that the trial has significantly changed the balance of power in Volpone and Mosca's relationship?

3 'The scene in which Volpone and Mosca plan their next ruse shows them united in their anticipation of the fun to come. However, one cannot but feel that Mosca has the most to gain, Volpone the most to lose.' Do you agree? Why do you think Volpone does not see the danger?

Scene 3

4 To what extent does Mosca dole out a kind of comic justice to each in this scene?

5 What does Mosca's treatment of the suitors show about him? Is he really play-acting?

6 How does Volpone aim to win back the suitors? Do you think his intention to taunt them first is a wise one? Why?

Scene 4

7 This scene has been the most criticised of the whole play. Is it possible to make it work on stage or is it doomed to fail?

8 Are the punishments of Sir Politic and his wife fitting? How?

Scene 5

9 What does Mosca's use of irony show about the relationship between him and Volpone?

10 Judging by his speech in lines 6–9, how does Mosca now see himself? Is he right to do so or is he making a mistake?

Scenes 6-9

11 Is it fitting that Volpone should have a chance to torture the legacy-hunters before they are finally punished by the court? Why?

How does he go about goading them in the scenes which follow?

Scene 10

12 What misjudgement have Volpone and Mosca made about Voltore? How does this throw them into crisis? What is different about the way they must face the danger this time?

13 Voltore speaks of 'conscience'. Is there an irony in this? How is his view of the world like Volpone's?

14 Why are Corvino and Corbaccio so inept at defending their interests?

Scene 12

15 Why does the first avocatore find the submission to be confusing?

16 What do the reactions and comments of the avocatori throughout this scene show about the nature of justice in Venice?

17 Is the scene in which Voltore fakes possession too ludicrous to work or has it got comic potential?

18 Why does Volpone choose to reveal himself when he knows it will bring punishment down upon him? How does Mosca immediately react and what does this show about him?

19 How convincing do you find the judges' words in lines 95–103?

20 In what state of mind is Volpone as he receives his punishment? Why do you think he should be like this?

Act 5 summary question

The first avocatore concludes the play with the words:

> Let all that see these vices thus rewarded,
> Take heart, and love to study 'em. Mischiefs feed
> Like beasts, till they be fat, and then they bleed.

Act 5, scene 12, lines 149–51

To what extent has it a 'happy ending'?

In performance

☐ There can be no better way to get to know a text than to prepare a scene from it as a rehearsal meeting and then to act it out. In rehearsal, your group should decide:

- the importance of the scene to the text as a whole;
- what you know of the characters already and how the scene adds to this knowledge;
- what the intended tone of the scene is to be – comic or serious;
- how characters are to speak their lines and react to each other, to events and to the audience in the scene;
- any cuts which may be needed;
- how to highlight key moments/speeches;
- how and where characters will move.

The next step is to rehearse the scene, walking through the movements, trying out ways of speaking and getting to know your character. It might help if one of the group acts as a director.

Finally, act it out to an audience and invite comments about the performance.

Good scenes to explore would be:

- The procession of suitors in Act 1.
- Volpone as the mountebank in Act 2, scene 2 and Corvino's interruption.
- Volpone and Mosca talking in Act 2, scene 4.
- Act 3, scene 7 – the attempted rape.
- The legacy-hunters testaments in Act 4, scene 5.
- Mosca in power in Act 5, scene 3.
- Sir Politic's fate in Act 5, scene 4.
- Voltore's possession in Act 5, scene 12.
- The climax of the play.

2 Explore the play from a director/producer's point of view:

- As a group, discuss the problems you would foresee in putting on a production of **Volpone** which would be popular today. Identify specific things (e.g. characters, themes, speeches, scenes) which would cause difficulties and come up with solutions.

- How would you go about selling the play to the local schools? Write the blurb which you would send out to
  - the teachers
  - the pupils.

  This may involve designing a suitable poster and promotional brochure.

- Because of the classical names used, a modern audience would be slow to pick up the animal imagery/jungle motif. How would you overcome this? Would you trust them to pick up the references or help them in terms of characters' dress, appearance or movement?

  Could programme notes help? If so, write some and see if they work.

- In a similar vein, how would you overcome the problems

which allusions to contemporary events or classical learning create? Would you cut these and, if so, what would the play lose?

- A modern audience, more politically correct than its Jacobean counterpart, might well be offended by the ridiculing of Corbaccio's infirmities, the rape scene or the portrayal of women in general in the play. Consider each issue in turn and decide what you would do about it.

- The sub-plot is a perceived weakness. Justify either leaving it in or omitting it from a production.

3 In this hot-seating activity, you take responsibility for researching a character and are then questioned, in role, by the rest of the group about actions, motives, beliefs etc. The value of the activity is that it makes you climb into a character's skin.

Choose the following characters to hot-seat.

- Volpone
- Mosca
- Corvino
- Voltore
- Celia

A variation of this would be for one student to research the character and aims of Ben Jonson and to be interrogated in that role. This should provoke a lively debate on his intentions and achievements.

Issues for debate

1 How does *Volpone* stand up to the poetic ideals propounded by Jonson in the Epistle?

2. Do you find the comedy surrounding Corbaccio's infirmities to be gratuitous or does it have a purpose?

3. Look at Mosca's character and actions carefully. Is there a point in Acts 1–4 where the motives behind his actions are clear or does he always play a double-handed game?

4. Volpone calls Mosca 'my redemption' (Act 2, scene 5; line 22). Is there an ironic truth in this?

5. Mosca says, 'Guilty men Suspect what they deserve still' (Act 3, scene 9, lines 20–1). How far does the fate of each character at the end of the play match their actions in it?

6. Would you agree that evil destroys itself at the end of the play or do you think that the ending has a more Christian message?

7. In Act 3, scene 9, line 18, Volpone tells Mosca that he is wise to 'the discovery of your tricks'. Why then does Mosca succeed in outwitting him later in the play?

8. To what extent do all of the characters contribute to their own downfall?

9. Support or oppose the inclusion of **Volpone** in examination set text lists.

Further assignments

Imagery

1. • In Act 3, scene 7, Volpone compares his passion for Celia to a banquet. Collect other examples of images of hunger and feeding being used for sensual lust. Analyse what each shows about the speaker.

- In Act 5, scene 3, line III, Volpone says to Mosca, 'Play the artificer now, torture 'em rarely.' Collect other examples where characters talk of play-acting to describe their behaviour. Analyse what each shows about the speaker.

- Other images to collect and analyse:
  - sickness and decay
  - gold
  - animalism.

Themes

2 Key themes in the play are:

- greed
- the disparity between appearance and reality
- parasitism
- delusion and self-delusion.

Trace the development of each, looking for key episodes in which they are explored.

Comedy

3 The hardest thing in the world is to describe why something is funny. A way around this is to categorise comedy into types and to provide examples of each.

Explore the use of the following types of comedy in Volpone:

- irony
- farce
- word-play
- routines surrounding a gull and a knave.

Are there any more? For all that you find, identify episodes which embody them.

Structure

4 Act 3, scenes 3–5 see a plot movement from crisis to despair to triumph which will be repeated throughout the play. Identify where this structure occurs and analyse the changes in it each time it is repeated.

Study questions

Context questions

This type of question is hard to do because of the depth of language study which it requires. Students often fall into the trap of writing in a generalised way when, in fact, the examiner wants them to use the context given as the starting point for *detailed* discussion of how language works, and what it shows about character and theme. The best advice is to practise as much as possible and to get used to analysing contexts virtually word by word.

Act I

1 Scene I (lines I–27) What does the passage show about the character of Volpone?

2 Scene I (lines 30–65) What does the justification given by Volpone and Mosca show about their characters?

3 Scene 3 (lines 51–74) How does Mosca use language both to tempt Voltore and to insult him in this extract?

Act 2

4 Scene 4 (lines 1–38) What does this extract show about the nature of Volpone's relationship with Mosca?

5 Scene 5 (lines 1–34) or (lines 45–72) What do we see of the character of Corvino and his relationship with his wife in this extract?

Act 3

6 Scene 7 (lines 28–58) or (lines 95–124) What do we see of the character of Corvino in this extract?

7 Scene 7 (lines 183–205) or (lines 206–235) How does Volpone try to seduce Celia?

8 Scene 7 (lines 240–275) What is the dramatic significance of this episode?

Act 4

9 Scene 5 (lines 29–59)

- How does this passage reflect Voltore's skill as a public speaker?
- What is the dramatic significance of this extract?

10 Scene 5 (lines 105–27) What do their responses show about the characters of Corvino and Corbaccio?

11 Scene 6 (lines 20–53) How does Voltore use rhetoric to defeat Bonario and fool the judges?

Act 5

12 Scene 11 (lines 1–22) What is the dramatic significance of this scene?

13 Scene 12 (lines 51–77)   How would you present this extract on stage?

Essay questions

Many of the activities you have already completed will help you to answer the following questions. Before you begin to write, consider these points about essay writing:

- Analyse what the question is asking. Do this by circling key words or phrases.

- Use each part of the question to 'brainstorm' ideas and references to the play which you think are relevant to the answer.

- Decide on the order in which you are going to tackle the parts of the question. It may help you to draw a flow-diagram of the parts so that you can see which aspects of the question are linked.

- Organise your ideas and quotations into sections to fit your flow-diagram. You can do this by placing notes in columns under the various headings.

- Write a first draft of your essay. Do not concern yourself too much with paragraphing and so on; just aim to get your ideas down on paper and do not be too critical of what you write.

- Redraft as many times as you need, ensuring all the time that:
  - each paragraph addresses the question;
  - each paragraph addresses a new part of the question, or at least develops a part;
  - you have an opening and closing paragraph which are clear and linked to the question set;
  - you have checked for spelling and other grammatical errors.

1 'What a rare punishment is avarice to itself!' Does the play bear out Mosca's judgement?

2 Celia says in Act 4, scene 5, line 102, 'I would I could forget I were a creature.' Does Jonson intend for us all to feel like this at

the end of the play or is there a note of optimism in its conclusion?

3 Mosca says of men:

> *Each of 'em*
> *Is so possessed, and stuffed with his own hopes,*
> *That anything unto the contrary,*
> *Never so true, or never so apparent,*
> *Never so palpable, they will resist it –*

Act 5, scene 2, lines 23–7

Does this explain not only his success but also, ironically, his
downfall?

4 Volpone describes Mosca as 'like a temptation of the devil'. Does
this capture his role in the play?

5 'I'm caught I' mine own noose – ' (Act 5, scene 10, lines 13–14).
How much is Volpone to blame for his own downfall?

6 'There is nothing comforting in the end of **Volpone**.' Discuss.

7 You are a teacher who receives a parental complaint about your
choice of **Volpone** as a study text. The parent feels that the text is
artistically flawed and immoral, in that it champions evil and ends
on a pessimistic note. Write a reply, defending the text against
these charges.

8 In an essay on **Volpone**, the actor Leo McKern argued that the
omission of Sir Politic Would-be would 'not materially affect the
mainstream of the plot'. Would you agree that the character is
superfluous to the play?

9 'Volpone both attracts and repels us: we are as fascinated by him
as by those we sneer at for being his victims.' Discuss.

10 'The image of Mosca as a fly does not quite work. He may be a parasite feeding upon corruption but there is nothing random in his actions.' Discuss.

11 Do we laugh *at* or *with* Volpone and Mosca?

12 'The ending is neither comic nor tragic, but a compromise of both. Nevertheless, its tone is in keeping with the play as a whole and so it works perfectly.' Discuss.

13 Eighteenth-century critics dismissed the play as being contrived and unrealistic. Do you agree with their judgement or does it sell Jonson's poetic achievement short?

14 Jonson claims in his Epistle that the great dramatist must also be a great poet. What are his poetic strengths as revealed in the play?

15 Venice is seen as a place of decay and disease. Trace the manifestations of both in the play.

16 'In *Volpone*, virtue is seen as a weakness.' Discuss.

17 'In many respects, Volpone is the model of the Renaissance man. This explains why we are so drawn to him.' Evaluate the character in the light of this comment.

Suggestions for further reading

In order to appreciate the traditions of Elizabethan and Jacobean comedy and tragedy, it is important to read Shakespeare and Marlowe as theirs is a skill more closely akin to Jonson's than his exact contemporaries'.

Comedy

Twelfth Night by William Shakespeare
This play is a study of human folly and contains a servant with aspirations above his station.

The Tempest and *Measure for Measure* by William Shakespeare
Both plays trace what happens when a man becomes too enraptured with power. Both are comedies with seeds of tragedy in them.

Tragedy

Othello by William Shakespeare
Othello's servant, Iago, is very much Mosca's tragic counterpart; a man with an endless appetite for treachery.

King Lear by William Shakespeare
The study of the disintegration of a man intoxicated with his own ego.

Dr Faustus by Christopher Marlowe
A scholar risks his soul to achieve his divine ambitions.

The Changeling by Thomas Middleton
A treacherous servant betrays all to satisfy his own lust.

If you want to read some more Jacobean comedy, try:
The Shoemaker's Holiday by Thomas Dekker
The Malcontent by John Marston
Philaster by John Fletcher
The Alchemist by Ben Jonson

Wider reading assignments

1. 'Be it through tragedy or comedy, Jonson and his contemporaries saw the chief aim of drama as being to instruct by exposing human weakness.' Comment on this statement.

2 'It was an age of artifice rather than realism.' Discuss this statement.

3 With reference to Jonson's **Volpone** and one of Shakespeare's plays, analyse what has proved timeless and universal about their characters and themes.

4 'A pleasure to study but painful to sit through.' Discuss this judgement with reference of **Volpone** and one other Elizabethan/Jacobean play.

5 'The message of the play is not that we will be saved by providence, but that evil will always destroy itself'. Discuss with detailed reference to two plays you have studied alongside **Volpone**.

Longman Literature

Series editor: Roy Blatchford

Novels

Jane Austen *Pride and Prejudice* 0 582 07720 6
Charlotte Brontë *Jane Eyre* 0 582 07719 2
Emily Brontë *Wuthering Heights* 0 582 07782 6
Anita Brookner *Hotel du Lac* 0 .582 25406 X
Marjorie Darke *A Question of Courage* 0 582 25395 0
Charles Dickens *A Christmas Carol* 0 582 23664 9
              Great Expectations 0 582 07783 4
              Hard Times 0 582 25407 8
George Eliot *Silas Marner* 0 582 23662 2
F Scott Fitzgerald *The Great Gatsby* 0 582 06023 0
                 Tender is the Night 0 582 09716 9
Nadine Gordimer *July's People* 0 582 06011 7
Graham Greene *The Captain and the Enemy* 0 582 06024 9
Thomas Hardy *Far from the Madding Crowd* 0 582 07788 5
            The Mayor of Casterbridge 0 582 22586 8
            Tess of the d'Urbervilles 0 582 09715 0
Susan Hill *The Mist in the Mirror* 0 582 25399 3
Aldous Huxley *Brave New World* 0 582 06016 8
Robin Jenkins *The Cone-Gatherers* 0 582 06017 6
Doris Lessing *The Fifth Child* 0 582 06021 4
Joan Lindsay *Picnic at Hanging Rock* 0 582 08174 2·
Bernard Mac Laverty *Lamb* 0 582 06557 7
Jan Mark *The Hillingdon Fox* 0 582 25985 1
Brian Moore *Lies of Silence* 0 582 08170 X
Beverley Naidoo *Chain of Fire* 0 582 25403 5
              Journey to Jo'burg 0 582 25402 7
George Orwell *Animal Farm* 0 582 06010 9
Alan Paton *Cry, the Beloved Country* 0 582 07787 7
Ruth Prawer Jhabvala *Heat and Dust* 0 582 25398 5
Paul Scott *Staying On* 0 582 07718 4
Virginia Woolf *To the Lighthouse* 0 582 09714 2

Short stories

Jeffrey Archer *A Twist in the Tale* 0 582 06022 2
Thomas Hardy *The Wessex Tales* 0 582 25405 1
Susan Hill *A Bit of Singing and Dancing* 0 582 09711 8
George Layton *A Northern Childhood* 0 582 25404 3
Bernard Mac Laverty *The Bernard Mac Laverty Collection* 0 582 08172 6

Poetry

Five Modern Poets edited by Barbara Bleiman 0 582 09713 4
Poems from Other Centuries edited by Adrian Tissier 0 582 22595 X
Poems in My Earphone collected by John Agard 0 582 22587 6
Poems One edited by Celeste Flower 0 582 25400 0
Poems Two edited by Paul Jordan & Julia Markus 0 582 25401 9

Longman Group Limited,
Longman House, Burnt Mill, Harlow,
Essex CM20 2JE, England
and Associated Companies throughout the world.

This educational edition first published 1995

Editorial material set in 10/12 point Gill Sans Light
Produced by Longman Singapore Publishers (Pte) Ltd
Printed in Singapore

ISBN 0 582 25408 6

The publisher's policy is to use paper manufactured from sustainable forests.

Cover illustration by John Bradley

Consultants: Geoff Barton and Jackie Head